W9-AQJ-320

THE PLAN

Also by Edwin Black

www.edwinblack.com

NAZI NEXUS
America's Corporate Connections to Hitler's Holocaust
www.nazinexus.com
2008

INTERNAL COMBUSTION
*How Corporations and Governments Addicted the World to Oil
and Derailed the Alternatives*
www.internalcombustionbook.com
2006

BANKING ON BAGHDAD
Inside Iraq's 7,000 Year History of War, Profit, and Conflict
www.bankingonbaghdad.com
2004

WAR AGAINST THE WEAK
Eugenics and America's Campaign to Create a Master Race
www.waragainsttheweak.com
2003

IBM AND THE HOLOCAUST
*The Strategic Alliance Between Nazi Germany
and America's Most Powerful Corporation*
www.ibmandtheholocaust.com
2001

THE TRANSFER AGREEMENT
*The Dramatic Story of the Pact Between the Third Reich
and Jewish Palestine*
www.transferagreement.com
1984 and 2001

FORMAT C: *A Novel*
www.formatnovel.com
1999

THE PLAN

How to Save America When the Oil Stops — or the Day Before

BY

EDWIN BLACK

DIALOG PRESS

WASHINGTON, D.C.

To my daughter Rachel, and future generations
I will never speak to but who may benefit
from the words written here.

THE PLAN. Copyright © 2008 by Edwin Black. All rights reserved.

No part of this publication may be reproduced, stored in a retrieval system, or transmitted in any form or by any means, electronic, mechanical, photocopying, recording, scanning, or otherwise, except as permitted under Section 107 or 108 of the 1976 United States Copyright Act, without either the prior written permission of the Publisher, or authorization through payment of the appropriate per-copy fee to the Copyright Clearance Center, Inc., 222 Rosewood Drive, Danvers, MA 01923, (978) 750-8400, fax (978) 646-8600, or on the web at www.copyright.com. Requests to the Publisher for permission should be addressed to permissions@dialogpress.com.

This book is printed on acid-free paper.

ISBN 978-091415307-8

Printed in the United States of America

12 11 10 09 08 5 4 3 2 1

Cover designed by Karl Kaufman

Any changes, corrections, or additions to this book can be found at http://www.planforoilcrisis.com

Contents

Acknowledgments

As always, when I embark upon great voyages of understanding, the ocean is filled with great vessels of assistance, indispensable fellow travelers, and not a few maelstroms to weather. One person cannot do this work without massive help. In all my projects, I have been blessed with great minds, energetic volunteers, and numerous individuals who opened doors and shined lights in the darkness at crucial moments. Their fingerprints are forever invisibly emblazoned along the margins and between the lines of every page of *The Plan*. But some of their names are also recited here.

I began the project with several dozen volunteers in seven countries assembling reams of data and documents in new and unusual ways to assemble the puzzle pieces of *The Plan*. But in the last several months, our battalion was reduced to a squad of day-in day-out researchers and fact checkers. First and foremost, I acknowledge team leader Annie Steinmetz in Arizona who worked tirelessly in spite of time zones and terrible computer crashes. Intellectual agility is the single most precious commodity in a project like this. She demonstrated it every day in fact checking, organizing, and project traffic supervision. Annie also showed her editorial prowess as the line editor. She became the fulcrum of the enterprise. There can only be one.

Martin Barillas in Michigan assisted with stubborn fact checking, assembling the documentation. As an editor in his own right, and a former diplomat, Martin brought great intellectual goods to the table. I also thank Eve Jones of New York for her keen eye, sharp editing and indefatigable energy in tackling footnotes and documentation. Because Eve has worked with me on several earlier books, she knew exactly what to do. Carol DiSalvo of Florida gave of her time during the most pivotal times on the project as the crunch times came. Eric Moore of New York assisted at a key moment of investigation as he tackled several pounds of data. Space does not permit me to list several dozen others from New Zealand, Canada, England, France and Israel who floated in and out of the project to volunteer at a crucial moment.

Each of my projects benefits from the vast knowledge, advice and mental clarity of many experts. I was blessed to have many with great insight representing both broad and narrow interests. Having worked with scores of scholars in this field, two of the most knowledgeable I have encountered are Gal Luft, Co-director of the Institute for the Analysis Global Security and Richard Kolodziej, Director of Natural Gas Vehicles America, who both assisted immeasurably.

Others who rendered detailed page and verse assistance include Erik Kreil of the Energy Information Administration of the Department of Energy, one of the nation's most devoted and knowledgeable oil crisis experts, along with his colleagues, Matt Cline and Mark Schipper. The Energy Information Administration (EIA) is the most important and underthanked energy agency in government, working with tireless devotion to protect this nation's energy vulnerability with its most potent secret weapon: *knowledge*. This agency is the bedrock of what America knows and does not know about the hole we are digging. The EIA operates numerous websites which are vast and reliable repositories of indispensable information. Anyone can access them day or night.

Likewise, I extend thanks to Jason Elliott of the International Energy Agency in Paris, a clear thinker whose information and insights were most valuable. Thanks to Karl Means and David Pordy of the Shulman Rogers law firm for their expertise regarding patent law.

My manuscript was tediously read and re-read in many versions on a deadline basis as we sculpted, balanced and harmonized the many competing interests, factual assertions, viewpoints and accumulated expertise. I give special thanks to Canadian oil expert Gord Laxer of the University of Alberta and the Parkland Institute, Norman Olsen of Iowa State University and the Iowa Energy Center, John Holbrook of the Ammonia Fuel Network, Mark Abramowitz of the California Hydrogen Business Center, and also to individuals I cannot name in the U.S. Department of Energy and the International Energy Agency who worked many hours to help my information be as correct as possible. I also thank Source A, Source B and Source C in the U.S. government who worked exhaustively with me on condition of anonymity and in so doing helped expose the awesome facts surrounding the nation's precarious sleep-walking deeper and deeper into the petroleum morass.

Numerous professional, commercial and corporate entities rendered pivotal assistance and deserve special commendation. Among the carmakers, I thank my personal favorite, Honda, for all it has done and shall do. Arguably the best of the manufacturers, Honda shall deliver. I have always driven Hondas and always will. Their executives exemplify some of the best thinkers on the planet.

An extra measure of gratitude goes to General Motors. In recent times, few have caused General Motors more public grief than I. In unending front page investigations, I have chronicled the company's conscious destruction of the electric trolleys, inexcusable alliance with Adolf Hitler, and seemingly intractable harm to our fuel independence. General Motors media relations people and their executives in the past have been arrogant and in denial about their own arrogance. Yet, knowing what they do about me, General Motors moved with electric speed to provide me every detail of information, every act of cooperation and access to its top executives. The company responded to every request--not within hours, days or weeks, but within minutes, sometimes moments. Perhaps this company has been reinvented from the inside out. Therefore unqualified and spotlighted thanks go to media manager Rob Peterson, GM Vice President Jon Lauckner and to Geri Lama as well as Source G and Source G1. On this book tour, I shall not only drive a Honda GX powered by CNG, but also a GM hydrogen vehicle. Perhaps on the next book tour, I will drive up in a GM Volt.

Salutes are given to the Canadian Association of Petroleum Producers. Its experts and media managers worked above and beyond with me, moment-to-moment on a deadline basis, to ensure that I had access to the most current and often still unpublished information. They did so without condition knowing that I oppose oil. Likewise, the Enbridge Corporation and the Canadian Energy Pipeline Association both mobilized all the information and insight at their disposal the moment I asked.

I was obstructed or otherwise refused information from a variety of important sources. The American Trucking Association declined to help and refused repeated requests for information. Shirley Neff of the Association of Oil Pipe Lines in Washington D.C. refused on several occasions to provide any information whatsoever. Without the complete helpfulness of the Enbridge Corporation and the Canadian Energy Pipeline Association, my understanding of how oil moves great distances would have been far less complete. The United States Holocaust Memorial Museum (USHMM) spurned all requests for information on General Motors and the Third Reich or on Nazi oil activities. The USHMM's four top executives, Andrew Hollinger, Paul Shapiro, Arthur Berger, Sara Bloomfield, already embattled for their bitter and protracted war with numerous Holocaust survivor organizations over information dissemination as well as critics seeking more insight into the Nazi-Arab alliance, declined to even respond to requests.

This project was enabled, in large measure, by software not previously available, or at least not in the configuration it now exists. At the top of the list is Adobe which provided my team with powerful suites permitting high-speed virtual information gathering, processing and assemblage. I also thank the Internet which, as bad as it is, can be an agent of immeasurable good.

Many have given me editorial assistance and endless supplies of encouragement. I include Elizabeth Black who took time from her own books to edit long distance, my daughter Rachel Black whose music moved me over all distances, and my father Harry Black who has already traveled enough distance to insure that I would persevere. My agent, Lynne Rabinoff, has always been there. The team at NBN, especially Spencer Gale and Jed Lyons, are inscribed for their support. To the production team at Dialog Press, especially production manager, Richard Farkas, nicknamed the Sheriff, I raise a glass. See this page with type on it—thank Richard. Likewise, our designer Karl Kaufman created a brilliant cover and related promotional materials in the few moments allotted to him. We acknowledge Angelique Cain for copy assistance. I also thank Gerry Terry for making sure the ink dried on time.

My team at *The Cutting Edge News,* an online publication at www.thecuttingedgenews.com, rendered great assistance every week for months. This includes at the top Ken Bobu in California and Uwe June in Germany, as well as Eduardo Szklarz in Argentina.

In every book, I acknowledge the music that has given me the inspiration to work numbing fifteen hour days for weeks at a time. The line-up this time includes John Powell for the Bourne trilogy, plus Hans Zimmer, DJ Lithium, Rachel Black for her work at myspace.com/rachelblackband, BT, Evanescence and Moby among others.

More thank you notes, information, and any manuscripts corrections shall be appended at www.planforoilcrisis.com, the interactive website for *The Plan.*

My final thanks go to all those who wake up and smell the oil then demand a breath of fresh air. The world needs change. Leaders will not do it despite their calling. Politicians will not despite their oratory. The media cannot take the time despite its duty. But the approaching crisis will create its own clock. If you have taken the time to learn the facts and wipe enough petroleum off your glasses that you can now see a path forward, I give you my greatest thanks. History will thank you as well.

Introduction

It was very distressing writing *The Plan*.

In recent years, I have authored books excavating the hidden history of persecution, genocide and injustice. These works include: *The Transfer Agreement* about the Nazi-Zionist negotiations during the Holocaust, *IBM and the Holocaust* revealing that company's twelve-year Holocaust planning project for the Third Reich, *War Against the Weak* documenting America's effort to create its own master race using the pseudoscience of eugenics and unleashing its own domestic genocide, *Banking on Baghdad* chronicling Iraq's bloody 7,000 year history of economic oppression and mass murder, and *Internal Combustion* which revealed exactly how society became addicted to oil.

Each of those works was two or three years in the making. When they sprang upon the public consciousness, timely yet timeless, the result was shockwaves of abrupt understanding. Headlines and public upset generated passionate discussion and debate. There was never a good time to reveal any of that information. Sometimes I dreaded telling the awful truth. Often the public dreaded hearing it. But my commitment was to reveal a dark history to help ensure a precious future.

This time it's different. My commitment is the opposite: reveal a dark future to help ensure a precious past. The "past" means life as we have known it. The "future" is life as it may become if our society remains addicted to oil, and if those who wish for the downfall of western society succeed in using our dependence as a weapon against us. This time the headlines and the revelations have preceded the book. My predictions became the daily punctuation of our lives. People could not wait to find a way out. Society needs a plan--an emergency plan--in the event the oil stops. No one has one. No one is even speaking of one. I could not wait to tell them. Every day as the situation worsened, my publishers and colleagues ask why the unfinished book could not come out the very next day.

But it was not always like that. In 2007, in the wake of *Internal Combustion*, my editors initially did not believe our nation would enter the type of oil crisis that I and many others were predicting.

Few could believe that a barrel of oil would double from 2007 to 2008 and even approach $150. But the price broke $147 a barrel in mid-July 2008. Everywhere the experts in 2008 predicted that oil would continue soaring past $200 per barrel and in essence go into permanent price escalation. Even when the prices dipped for a few days, the prospect of diminishing supply, mushrooming global demand and threatening geopolitical and petropolitical disruptions revealed oil for what it was: an economically out of control commodity that the world required every hour of every day. Without it, modern society would collapse.

Few in 2007 could believe the world might be beset by food riots and that we would see the meteoric rise of food prices even in the capitals of industrialized cities. But that happened as basic food stuffs and the cost of transporting them escalated everywhere causing food panics from Mexico City to Minneapolis to Milan. Mexicans raised an uproar about the high cost of corn for tortillas. Italians protested the price of pasta. Americans began hording rice at Sam's Club. In Third World and emerging countries, unrest over food shortages and increased prices boiled over before TV cameras. The quiet suggestions of the experts quickly became a phenomenon of the nightly news.

Few in 2007 could believe that the supply chokepoints were as narrow as they are. No one understood where our oil came from or how easy it was to disrupt. Then the media began examining this puzzle piece by piece. People began seeing just how vulnerable the modern world has become. We are very tall and can topple easily.

Yet for all the pain and predictions suffered by America and the world due to petroleum, no one has yet asked three questions: 1) How much of a stoppage would be required to throw our nation into chaos? 2) Exactly what could cause that? 3) What does society do if it really happens? Is there no plan?

Certainly, the experts have been trying to run computer models and even theoretical practice runs, such as "Operation Shockwave" which in 2005 brought national security and oil experts together in a Washington Hotel to simulate a protracted oil disruption. The results were panic and pain. "The American people are going to pay a terrible price for not having had an energy strategy," said former CIA director Robert M. Gates shortly after the exercise. Gates had assumed the character of "national security adviser" for the 2005 practice run. Shockwave's results were a terrifying presage of what society could endure without warning. "The scenarios portrayed were absolutely not alarmist," explain Gates. "They're realistic."

Yet while the experts could wring their hands over how oil could disrupt and perhaps devastate society, no one could create a plan to cope with such an event. For this reason, I have written *The Plan*. While the book pretends to be a crisis plan, don't be fooled. This needs to be implemented immediately. Without preparedness, no plan can hope to do anything but ease the pain.

In assembling my information, I was careful to consult numerous other plans and precedents drawing on the strong points of many alternatives. In doing so, I discovered that the field of oil crisis solutions is filled not just with "single-issue" pressure groups, but with "single-sentence" pressure groups. As I produced my work, so many were intent on lobbying for their specific sentence and solution: electric, more oil, ethanol of any flavor, compressed natural gas (CNG), ammonia, hydrogen, biodiesel, flex-fuel, rotted and re-used materials of all descriptions, and bacteria of many types. For this reason, I became convinced that even the experts do little more than become expert in their own expertise to the exclusion of every other idea.

In truth, there is no one truth to solve our vulnerability. There is no magic bullet. But there is a barrage of ideas and strategies that can come together, cutting across all the entrenched positions to create the plan we need. We need a plan to get off of oil—and quickly—in the event of a crisis. That crisis could come the day you read this information or years later. But the day will come.

Because of the extremely volatile nature of the information and the suggestions, I wish to take this opportunity to repeat the admonishment I have inserted in the Introduction of each of my last six books. *The Plan* is not to be read in snatches. If you cannot read the book in its entirety, front to back, without skipping around, please don't read it at all. Context is needed. The energy crisis is filled with misinformation disseminated by paid partisans, well-meaning pundits and marginally informed mavens, only to be proliferated as expertise by a frenzied media which operates only catchphrase deep.

The reality is if you are reading this at all, the situation is not good. *The Plan* is not a book of entertainment. It is a crisis manual. Does *the Plan* have all the answers? Of course not, and does not pretend to. But it has enough answers to prompt further questions as each person and locality finds a way to survive an unexpected oil stoppage.

Can we do it? Answer: I am not sure. If we start now, how long will it take? Answer: Years. But there is no hope without a plan. Now we have one.

Edwin Black
www.edwinblack.com
Washington, D.C.
August 20, 2008

CHAPTER ONE

There is No Plan

When the oil stops, the news will appear like a mushroom cloud in the distance, towering and terrifying, yet intangible. But like a fiery orange atomic explosion unfurling in slow motion, the concussive blast will soon reach us all. Then, the fallout will hit in protracted waves of misery.

First the trucks and shippers will curtail shipments. Shelves will become scant and in some cases bare. Quickly, unemployment will become epidemic as people are laid off due to economic contraction or because many will simply be unable to get to work. That in turn will worsen the country's economic convulsion. Mobile America will cease to exist as we knew it because transportation via automobiles, taxis, buses, planes and other vehicular traffic will become an ever more unaffordable luxury. When people cannot get from Point A to Point B, the nation's economic vitality will quickly wither. Sudden pauperization—loss of employment, savings and home—will follow for whole sectors of an already teetering society as surely as it did during the ravages of Fascism, which systemically took everything—from the vulnerable first, then from almost everyone else.

Food shortages for many, and starvation for humanity's fringe, will appear as a ghastly consequence of the new times. The harvesting and shipping of food will escalate in cost, and that escalation will become turbo-charged as more and more farm acreage is diverted to biofuels. Rather than a bogey-man prediction, the specter of food riots worldwide became real in late 2007 when Jacques Diouf, director-general of the UN's Food and Agriculture Organization, declared, "If prices continue to rise, I would not be surprised if we began to see food riots."[1]

During the preparation of this chapter, ominous predictions based on underreported, almost obscure, international developments suddenly became outstripped by tornadic daily events proving the point and accelerating the crisis. Over-the-horizon notions foreshadowed in 2007 became a scream from the rooftops and the stuff of nightly newscast headlines. By spring 2008, biofuels-blamed food staple riots requiring armed government suppression had already broken out in at least 15 nations including Russia, Mexico, El Salvador, Haiti, Egypt, Bangladesh, Thailand and several African states. Mass starvation due to fuel-stoked food prices suddenly loomed on a scale not previously seen in dozens of countries for an estimated 100 million people. Numerous nations began formulating countermeasures to fuel-based food riots, including governmental bodies in the Philippines, India and even such stable societies as Australia, France, the United Kingdom and the United States.[2]

Indeed, during April 2008, the crisis hit home even in the well-fed USA. Leading "buy in bulk" retailers, such as Costco and Sam's Club, suddenly announced rice rationing, in some stores voluntary and in some units enforced. Nonetheless, some stores actually reported food shortages. At the same time, food banks for the disadvantaged reported angry citizens waiting in line for depleted supplies.[3] Publishers and distributors spoke of prominently placing this book not only in conventional bookstores but in thousands of grocery stores around the nation as the entire topic was now more than merely political or environmental fodder for the mind, but indeed a matter of food and household necessity.

British Prime Minister Gordon Brown called biofuel-related starvation a greater threat to world stability than the international credit crunch surging through the money-wracked world of 2008. "Tackling hunger," Brown declared, "is a moral challenge to each of us and it is also a threat to the political and economic stability of nations." World Food Program executive director Josette Sheeran agreed, terming the "food or fuel" crisis a "silent tsunami." Jean Ziegler, the U.N.'s ranking food official made headlines worldwide by going so far as to declare to a German radio station that "Producing biofuels today is a crime against humanity." India's finance minister used the same words in condemning the trend to corn ethanol.[4]

Surely many will die if the oil stops or is radically reduced. Large numbers will simply slip quietly into death from weakness and malnutrition. But how many will also die fighting as the aggression between men heightens in the face of a shrinking food supply? If a man must choose to pump a gallon of gas to secure a gallon of milk for his babies, he will. As society spirals down into desperation, who will be blamed? What hoarders will be shot? How many will carjack a vehicle not for its stereo but for its gasoline? How many will jump a fence to drill a gas tank? Which gas stations will be overrun? How many will never get to the hospital in an emergency? How many buildings will burn because fire trucks cannot roll for lack of fuel?

The situation can get worse if an oil shortage becomes intractable. Rooftop ethanol stills producing stockaded "moonshine fuel" will become a fact of life complete with the armed motorcycle marauders who populate "future shock" movies. They will jump from the screen into our communities.

War for oil will result. The blood of young men mixing with the ooze of oil will once again drain the life out of industrialized nations as it has so many times during the turbulent 20th century and the first groans of the tower-tumbled 21st century. Those who crave the oil will fight to get it. Those who possess it will fight to withhold it.

All the nightmare scenarios have been written, published, broadcast, epistled, door hammered, lectured and Web-spread throughout the hemispheres and blogospheres and the tired ears of a helpless world. That world wonders if it should act up and demand, look up and beseech, or just give up and wait. We get the message: Oil is our necessity and our curse. All of us have heard some of it, all of it, too much of it.

Understandably, therefore, if the oil stops, panic indeed will be the first chemical reaction of the masses. It should not be, and need not be. Like any snow emergency, water drought or natural disaster, a national oil supply emergency should be governed by a plan.

A Plan? America does not have such a plan. No Plan A. No Plan B.

But it should. Of all the worrisome words and perilous predictions reverberating within our collective consciousness, the one thing the world is still missing is a real plan.

Now it has one.

CHAPTER TWO
_____

Crude Realities

First, we must understand: Exactly what could cause a physical oil shortage or other debilitating fuel disruption? While the system is so fragile that any slight shock such as a refinery fire or pipeline accident could produce a measurable shortage, the shortfall would undoubtedly be brief. Global oil supplies would recover, after a round of convenient price spikes. The real threat is a long-term blockage or disruption.

Most people have heard of the oft-mentioned threats, such as hurricanes or terrorism. But many threats are misunderstood or exaggerated—even by the experts, and especially by the media. Moreover, most people don't have a real understanding of how America gets it oil, who uses it, who supplies it, and under what circumstances. From individual consumers to great corporations, from cities and states to the federal government, public or private, we are all completely dependent upon petroleum. Yet few understand the crude realities.

The facts of oil supply and demand are alternately obscure and confusing to most, and deceptively oversimplified by many. It starts with the old cliché about oil being globally *fungible*.[1]

In other words, the global market is just that: global. An oil supply or demand development anywhere on the planet can affect every other supply or demand source on the planet. Extra consumption in Kiev or Calcutta can affect in real time the availability and pricing in Kansas or California. Extra supply in Poland or Norway can relieve the moment-to-moment pressure on truck drivers in Pennsylvania or Nebraska.

That said, the pure fungibility of global oil can be thwarted by petropolitical havoc or market intervention, such as boycotts and embargoes, price increases designed to wage economic warfare, calculated diversions and shutdowns, regional issues, and rapacious oil industry manipulations. If the Arabs withhold oil in retaliation for some Western political act, if Venezuela diverts their output from America to China, if Western Canadian oil interests deliberately choose to ship their oil to Asia and not to Montreal, requiring Eastern Canada to import petroleum from the Middle East, the dynamics will be felt both on the global markets and in all localities.

As confusing as it is, the truth is this: Oil is indeed fungible—*but not always*, because oil supply and demand have always been manipulated by the powers that be. Whether it was the criminal oil market fraud of the late 19th century Rockefeller and Flagler business empires, the Allied denial of fuel to the Nazis during World War II, the Arab boycott of Israel's oil needs, the Arab oil embargo of 1973 or America's ban on oil imports from Libya and Iran, governments and magnates have proven they can subvert the free market fungibility of oil and at will create calculated gluts or droughts.

SUPPLY AND DEMAND

Some numbers are needed. The world devours some 86 million barrels of oil daily, as of the summer of 2008. That number grows continuously. Crude production, as of 2008, generally slimmed to only about 500 thousand to 1 million barrels per day above demand levels. Hence the international system of production and distribution contains very little cushion for normal day-to-day disruptions, such as industrial accidents, infrastructure disruptions or natural disasters. As worldwide demand continues to grow—an estimated 2-3 percent annually, more than 40 percent of that growth from the newly industrializing and modernizing nations of Asia—production increases just barely keep pace.[2]

Soon, the oil supply-to-demand ratio will lose its cushion or even become outstripped. At the point when demand completely exceeds production—whether that occurs by 2015 or 2030, depending upon prognostication—the extended Middle East will possess the dominant remaining reserves. That condition will only magnify the West's utter dependence upon that troubled region's cooperation for day-to-day existence.[3]

It would be wrong to focus too much on "reserves" or "peak oil," both of which are theoretical and misleading. More relevant is the escalating day-to-day global demand, which will actually outpace day-to-day global production. For the average citizen, oil will "peak" not the decade that so many wells run dry, or the year a statistician's "daily demand curve" exceeds daily drilling. It will "peak" the very hour a person cannot pump a gallon of gas or buy bread on an unstocked supermarket shelf because someone thousands of miles away has cut the lines of supply.

Each hour brings us closer and closer to that moment.

Every time an impoverished African nation builds a two-lane road to help starving farmers, every time a family in Peru gathers enough wealth to purchase their first car, every time a Chinese businessman installs another noisy diesel generator to supplement flagging electrical power, every time a California developer builds a new home in the exurbs of San Diego requiring a longer commute, every time a Polish entrepreneur opens a new store, humanity requires more oil to make it work.[4]

As the world modernizes and industrializes—*as it must*... as the world rescues more populations from the brink of famine and isolation—*as it must*... as society proliferates the intelligent use of fertilizers and pharmaceuticals to improve crop yields and cure illnesses everywhere—*as it must*, the pivotal lubricant is petroleum. Oil has become the very oxygen of progress.

In its highly prodigious role, the United States, as of early 2008, consumed more than 22 million barrels of crude oil daily, and that figure is bulging upward continuously. About 63 percent of America's oil goes for transportation, mainly for passenger cars, but sizable consumption is also attributed to trucks, boats, airplanes, mass transit, specialty vehicles and related transport. Increasingly, more than half the nation's crude is imported—more than 11 million barrels daily.[5]

If this book is read on any given Monday, the level of imports will be enormous. If the book is read just a week later, the numbers may be even larger. By the time all the chapters are read, all numbers may be vastly greater. That is the high-velocity nature of oil consumption.

This country's big five foreign suppliers, as of summer 2008, are listed as: Canada first and foremost at some 2 million barrels daily, followed by Saudi Arabia at more than 1.5 million barrels daily, Mexico at about 1.4 million barrels daily, and then Venezuela and Nigeria each with approximately 1.2 million barrels daily. The remainder comes from a collection of OPEC oil states such as Iraq and Kuwait, as well as such troubled non-OPEC countries as Russia and Chad, plus some of our best allies, such as Great Britain and Norway. These numbers, like all oil demand numbers, increase weekly.[6]

But who is really supplying America?

Despite the apparent foreign suppliers, no one should think that national borders or identities really define the true source of oil. Names, logos and flags mean nothing when they are emblazoned across an oil barrel. From the first years of the 20th century, thousands of oil company subsidiaries scattered across the world, each with localized national names, have masked true foreign ownership. British Petroleum itself was a small German company distributing kerosene in the United Kingdom until it was seized by England as enemy property during the first throes of WWI. It was merged into Britain's sprawling Anglo-Persian Oil Company, which was then renamed "British Petroleum." During those same early 20th Century years, the Asiatic Petroleum Company was hardly an Asian company. It was instead a joint venture operated by the Royal Dutch Petroleum Company of Amsterdam and Shell Transport and Trading of London, which became the 60-40 conglomerate known as Shell Oil. The American Gasoline Company pumping oil in Oklahoma in 1912 was no U.S. firm but was in fact owned and operated by that same Dutch-British venture that became Shell.[7]

Indeed, Shell's early 20th century organizational chart, sleepily reposing in company archives, shows more than 1,100 locally named subsidiaries around the world existed even then, all controlled by Dutch and British interests. The same approach rules today. For example, the PetroKazakhstan Oil Company of Central Asia, producing some 150,000 barrels of Kazak oil, is not a native enterprise; rather, it is a Canadian firm—or was until late 2005. Still headquartered in Calgary, the Canadian firm was subject to a $4.2 billion stock takeover by Chinese investors who beat an Indian oil concern also vying for the company. Hence the Kazak enterprise is in fact owned by a Canadian company controlled by the Chinese.[8]

The planet is littered with similar oil companies bearing localized monikers but in truth owned by foreigners, with many pumping seemingly localized crude that is in fact re-exported from elsewhere.

National identity labels, logos and seeming points of origin not only disguise the realities of supply, but a worldwide maze of these façades camouflages the international implications. That becomes doubly important since virtually every expert argues that the global oil supply is indeed inherently fungible. As a result, new questions about the fungible dimension of supply are raised when one considers America's number one source of imported oil: Canada.

While oil experts and critics incessantly focus on the volatile Mideast, parsing the petroleum facts and rightly so, the foreign oil supply next door—more than 2 million barrels per day—is misunderstood. Too many wrongly take Canadian oil for granted as a cornerstone of America's economic survival.

CANADA—THE REALITIES AND THE RISK

Canada is a so-called *net oil exporter*, meaning it produces more petroleum than it consumes. As of 2008, almost all its excess crude is piped in from the province of Alberta to such Midwestern and northern American states as Illinois, Minnesota and Wisconsin, according to the Canadian Association of Petroleum Producers. On its face, that seems reassuring to Americans worried about a potential stoppage. America's number one foreign supplier is the friendly nation to the north, Canada.[9]

But looking deeper, it becomes clear that Canada is not just shipping 2 million barrels per day down to the U.S. There is more to the story. The numbers can be confusing since they are reported in various volumetric forms and quantities to various national and international energy agencies. Experts on Canadian oil may differ. But the best numbers from Canadian petroleum industry and government sources show a complex, layered picture that impacts every American.

That picture reveals that Canada is not just shipping some 2 million barrels per day to the U.S., Canada is also *importing* about 850,000 barrels each day from a variety of foreign sources, including Iraq, Saudi Arabia, Algeria, Egypt, Venezuela, as well as the United Kingdom, Norway and other countries. These imports come across the ocean in an endless stream of tankers unloading in Eastern Canada. As of August 2007, Canadian government numbers reflected 102,000 barrels daily from Algeria, 89,000 from Iraq, 76,000 from Saudi Arabia, plus Venezuela's 62,000 and additional imports from other OPEC nations.[10]

Beyond the OPEC nations, official Canadian numbers submitted to international oil agencies also show such European sources as Italy with 14,000 barrels daily and France with 25,000 barrels daily.[11]

Italy and France? Those countries export olive oil, not crude oil. Italy, for example, imports virtually all of its petroleum, more than 2 million barrels daily, as of summer 2008. Almost all of Italy's oil comes from Libya, Saudi Arabia, Iran, Iraq and other OPEC or Arab states. It exports refined OPEC product to Canada and other destinations. France imports an amount of oil almost equal to Italy, and once again almost of it from OPEC countries, chiefly Iran, Iraq, and Saudi Arabia, as well as Libya, Angola, and Algeria. The French then export some refined products.[12]

Hence, citizens of two countries are misled. The United States rests assured that a significant supply of its imported oil is coming from Canada. Eastern Canadians either don't know where their oil is coming from or rest assured that their imported supply comes from numerous sources in Europe in addition to the known OPEC countries. But, in fact, such countries as France and Italy simply pass on the refined oil obtained from OPEC, the Mideast and other troubled nations. Indeed, it is not clear exactly how much oil is coming from where since so much is reflagged, re-exported or passed through a conduit on a fungible basis. No wonder an August 2007 Canadian government report on the oil trade listed 78,000 barrels of its daily imports as "Not Elsewhere Specified" among a long list of several dozen countries from Australia to Zaire.[13]

If the OPEC alliance stems its flow, that stoppage will affect the world's interdependent distribution channels, encompassing Europe, Canada and the United States.

Moreover, even the oil produced on Canadian territory is less than a sure, eternal supply. True, several new cross-border pipelines designed to increase flow are now in development. True, investors are colliding at the door, rushing to expand, accelerate and capitalize on every precious barrel of petroleum. But Canadian oil is at best a problematic and increasingly debated resource. Indeed, the whole idea of intensified dependence upon the long-time Canadian oil partner is a rather recent development.

Approximately 95 percent of Canada's massive 180 billion barrel reserve is based on Alberta oil sands, also known as *tar sand*. "Tar sand" is actually a misnomer since tar is a manufactured concoction and the tar in Alberta's fields is actually the precious oily goop embedded within the sands. That goop is very difficult to extract. In fact, until recent technological advances and economic barriers were broken, tar sands were not even considered a viable source of oil. The very idea of extracting oil from tar sand was such an extreme notion that Alberta's deposits were not even included in the international annals of world global oil reserves. For decades, the Canadian government and industry debated whether large scale extraction was even realistic. But after the Arab Oil Embargo of 1973, a new economic oil order was inaugurated, new technologies came to the fore, and new levels of ecological destruction became palatable. Yet, even then, the cost of extraction was still high, even as many tar sands projects continued to yield valuable oil.[14]

What changed everything? Only in 2003—at about the time of the U.S. invasion of Iraq—were Alberta tar sands suddenly declared cost-effective and part of the revised global supply. Instantaneously, the international assessment of Canadian oil reserve astronomically zoomed from less than 10 billion barrels to 180 billion barrels— thus overnight becoming the second greatest recognized oil reserve on the planet after Saudi deposits.[15] In effect, the flash addition of Canadian tar sands inflated the shaky earth upon which the entire concept of global peak oil is based.

But a gathering storm of Canadian environmentalist opposition is determined to curtail that country's high-velocity multibillion-dollar tar sand production. In early 2008, one of a crop of newly hatched Canadian environmental groups issued a special study entitled "The Most Destructive Project on Earth," which dubbed tar sand extraction "a slow motion oil spill" larger than the Exxon Valdez. Industry reports concede the dimensions of the environmental impact. These industry reports confirm that about two tons of tar sand–laden earth must be "strip mined" to extract a single barrel of oil. A diverse array of oil extraction and processing methods all require massive volumes of natural gas and water, depleting two precious natural resources that will not be replenished.[16]

Critics charge that the 24/7 process wreaks havoc on the landscape, drains the water table, and produces a gargantuan source of greenhouse gases. Industry rebuts that its new recycling technology and use of brackish sources addresses the water problem. Opponents add that the extremely toxic and resource-intensive nature of extracting tar sands has created one of the world's largest dams, this for the sole purpose of storing poisonous byproducts. Rivers are being polluted not as much through runoff as ground seepage and other disposal techniques. Acid rain percolated from this industry afflicts parts of Canada far distant from the mines.[17]

Canada's oil sand region—a land mass about the size of Florida—is being destroyed before the world's eyes, critics say. Many Canadians—some say a small, but vocal group—have woken up to this growing crisis and are speaking out.

Since some 75 percent of Canada's oil production is devoted to

America's growing consumption, with the cross-border export level growing every day, Canadian opponents have called their country what one prominent critic labels a newly established "resource colony" or "energy satellite" of the United States. This notion is only underscored by Article 605 of the North American Free Trade Agreement, popularly known as NAFTA, which virtually compels Canada to export its oil to the United States at the same level that it has for any prior three-year period. Article 605 declares that Canada can impose an export restriction only so long as "the restriction does not reduce the proportion of the total export shipments of a specific energy or basic petrochemical good made available to such other Party... in the most recent 36-month period... prior to the imposition of the measure." The United States is the only other "Party" since Mexico too is a net exporter. Even the price Canada charges to the U.S. comes under the treaty's scope. As Canada increases its exports to the U.S., the lopsided treaty virtually assures that, subject to market fluctuations, Canada cannot substantially curtail cross-border sales for its own use in the event of an emergency or special need, without U.S. consent.[18]

Hence, Canada maintains its own petropolitical dynamic, just as do Venezuela and Iran, albeit for dramatically different and distinctly westernized national reasons. As a result, the petropolitical movement in Canada, along with rising insecurities about the sureness of Eastern Canada's true oil supply and a surging environmental worry, has already yielded a real impact.

First, the important pipeline flow from Sarnia to Montreal, known as Enbridge Line 9, is expected to be reversed—this for reasons of energy self-sufficiency, and simple commercial sense. Oil pipelines are like railroads. They simply carry the crude or refined products that oil shippers and customers consume. Pipelines can flow in either direction once the proper pumping adjustments are made. Such reversions can cost tens of millions of dollars. Originally built in the 1970s after the first Arab Oil Embargo, the 30-inch Line 9 pipeline allowed Western Canadian oil from Alberta transported into the American Great Lakes region to reconnect back up to Canada. This supplied Eastern Canada with its own oil via this long U-shaped bi-national route. In 1999, the direction of that flow was reversed. Canada then began shipping its imported oil from Montreal to Sarnia and from there trucked refined products across the border into America, according to the Canadian Association of Petroleum Producers. Line 9, as of summer 2008, carries between 125,000 and 134,000 barrels of imported crude per day to Canadian refineries, although the line has greater capacity. Those refineries then send finished oil products into the U.S. The supply is vital to America's northeast.[19]

With incessant spikes in oil prices and some awareness of their own vulnerability to Mideast petropolitical developments and terrorism, Canadian citizens and business have argued that Line 9's flow must be reverted back to Canada. This may occur as early as 2010, according to the Canadian Association of Petroleum Producers and other oil sources. That will increase Canadian access to its own oil. Canada's oil industry asserts its growth will be enough to supply both sides of the Northeast border. But others assert the reversion cannot help but reduce American availability to the imported overseas crude transported through Canada as a conduit.[20]

Second, the same concern that others have about Mideast petropolitics and terrorism has resulted in a vocal move by Canadians for their own Strategic Petroleum Reserve. Most industrial nations maintain a Strategic Petroleum Reserve (SPR) both for their own home-grown preparedness and because of international security treaty obligations to share stockpiles in the event of an oil shortage. A loophole in Canada's oil security treaty obligations, based on its *net exporter status,* allows that nation to function without any SPR. That loophole as well as the monumental Alberta deposits also yields a governmental mindset that believes the nation does not actually need such a reserve. But Canadian citizen groups, commentators and legislators believe the time has come. An SPR in Canada is more than possible. The same type of deep salt cavern structures that serve as strategic petroleum reserves along the American Gulf Coast exist near Sarnia, one of Canada's main petrochemical hubs. Eventually, the need for a Canadian SPR may materialize. Should Canada begin filling an SPR from its own domestic sources, that diversion will also put pressure on supplies to the U.S., a fact acknowledged by oil industry analysts on both sides of the border.[21]

Third, rising upset over NAFTA's compulsory export provisions is only reinforcing domestic Canadian unhappiness over increasing oil sales south of its border. True, the irresistible lure of billions in oil money from America has ruled the course of Canadian oil policy. But a rising tide of concern maintains the deeper national cost of those petrodollars will be too high since each additional barrel exported to America mandates an ever higher obligation that cannot be reversed according to NAFTA—this at the expense of Canadian interests.

Fourth, the angry environmental objections to Alberta's destructive tar sand production have already yielded the first major governmental restrictions, including one that all tar sand operations achieve zero carbon emissions beginning 2012. While these are the first such restrictions in North America, most say they are not the last. Critics assert that there are numerous spacious loopholes around this first set of environmental restrictions. But the advent of any new rules at all shows that the Canadian government finds domestic environmental protest a roiling issue it must deal with. Most observers in and out of government believe that more environmental restrictions are on the way.[22]

Fifth, the same oil rush frenzy that keeps Canada's production levels at peak acceleration despite nationalistic, environmental and political opposition has taken a new dollar-driven turn. Canadian oilmen have realized that the U.S. is not the only nation desperate for Alberta's crude. China wants it. To that end, the Chinese have purchased controlling stakes in several key Canadian oil exploration and production companies. Moreover, Chinese companies have become cheap and therefore economically enabling manufacturers' outsourcing arm for many Canadian oil enterprises.[23]

In the last months of 2007, China's appetite for oil soared with suddenly regular purchases of Canadian crude, which from June to September 2007 totaled 3.4 million barrels, sometimes as much as 49,000 barrels per day. By December 2007, three Chinese refineries were geared up for continuous Canadian oil shipments. By the summer of 2008, Canada's Enbridge Pipeline Co. had organized $4 billion to revive a shelved idea for a 720-mile pipeline from Alberta to a deep water port in British Columbia in order to ensure a massive daily supply of crude for Asia-bound tankers. The so-called Gateway Pipeline is planned to pump not the 49,000 barrels per day that China was buying in summer 2008 but nearly ten times as much—400,000 barrels per day—for China and other Asian customers such as Chinese Hong Kong. This substantial volume is planned to flow as soon as 2014.[24]

Americans take the suddenly ascendant Canadian oil supply for granted as the lynchpin of its energy survival. Canadians have become aware that their pivotal oil riches are gushing in a fashion that is problematic at best. Increasingly, Canadians feel it is a gusher that should not be taken for granted. Indeed, if Eastern Canada's Mideast supply is curtailed, critics argue that some of the volume Alberta is sending to the United States may be needed elsewhere in Canada.

MEXICO—A DIMINISHING RESOURCE

America's number three supplier after Canada and Saudi Arabia is providing 1.4 million barrels of oil per day—but for how much longer? In plain words, Mexico is quickly reaching Hubbert's Peak, the moment when oil production has depleted the majority of the reserve and the field has become a dwindling resource. Pemex, Mexico's national oil company, was created in 1938 out of the remnants of Dutch, American and British global petroleum interests. Most of its production is pumped from the four oilfields that comprise the Cantarell complex situated off the Bay of Campeche. Once thought to contain an estimated 35 billion barrels of oil, geologists realized only 18 billion barrels could be drilled due to encroaching water and gas. At the turn of the 21st Century, reserves were thought to be sufficient for 20 more years. By 2003, new techniques such as nitrogen injection escalated Cantarell production to 2.1 million barrels per day. But in 2006, the news spread that Mexican officials and executives had lied and the wells were expected to run dry in one decade not two.[25]

By April 2008, exports had dropped almost 12.5 percent for the first quarter of the year, and production dropped 7.8 percent to below 3 million barrels daily for the first time since the 2003 surge. Industry analysts worldwide predicted Mexico would run dry by 2017, and until then would export less and less as it covered its own domestic energy needs. Mexico itself consumes some 2 million barrels per day.[26]

More than running out of oil from existing reserves, Pemex has been essentially bankrupt for years, preventing further finds. Despite the seeming wealth it should possess, Pemex has been able to operate only by gargantuan borrowing. Even with more than $77 billion in annual revenues, by summer 2008, the company was more than $50 billion dollars in debt. That economic shambles arose due to a combination of massive corruption and skims, the after effects of numerous oil spills—including Ixtoc I, the biggest oil spill disaster in history—and the main reason: mandated revenue diversion. Some 60 percent of Pemex's income is given to the government to pay for some 30 to 40 percent of Mexico's annual national budget.[27]

Pemex is Mexico's cash cow. But the cow is now mere skin and bones. Pemex doesn't have the budget or foreign investment to extend its fast dwindling reserves or to drill for the new and challenging deposits below the Gulf of Mexico. Such new drilling would require the equivalent of tens of billions of dollars. Plans to re-privatize Pemex are politically explosive.[28] Many international oil interests would be financially better off if Mexico were simply subtracted from the global oil equation, thus making every other barrel of oil in the world that much more precious and costly. That subtraction could come in five years, perhaps less.

A wild card is the continued domestic terrorism waged against oil pipelines by such Mexican insurgent groups as Popular Revolutionary Army (EPR), which in July 2007 detonated a string of catastrophic pipeline explosions in Veracruz and elsewhere. The government dispatched 5,000 troops to guard the lines but the

EPR has proven their ability to bomb both remote and urban locations at will. The armed revolutionary group released a video vowing further destruction if Pemex were privatized.[29]

THREATENING THE HOUSE OF CARDS

The Canadian and Mexican supply channels—our number one and number three foreign sources—are just two aces in the house of cards that constitute America's tenuous 60 percent imported petroleum dependency. That house of cards can be toppled with very little vibration because global production itself is no longer large enough to cushion itself from protracted disruptions.

Indeed, a fire in early February 2008 at one small Texas refinery in Big Spring, Texas, which processes a mere 70,000 barrels per day, caused a nervous twitch in the world's global supply price precisely because the world's distribution is so hard-pressed to absorb even routine disruption. By early April 2008, only half production had been restored at the Big Spring, Texas, facility, but additional industrial accidents at the plant delayed full refining for many months.[30]

The point is: If so small a disruption can turn the heads of oil supply analysts worldwide, what would happen in the event of a major supply disruption? What could cause such a disruption? How much vibration would be needed to bring down the house of cards?

The truth is far more granulated than media "scare tacticians" would have us believe. The system, fragile as it is, has nonetheless until now been resilient enough to recover from incessant industrial accidents such as fires and spillages, as well as Gulf hurricanes and terrifying, platform-jarring seas, and from terrorist pinpricks such as isolated pipeline explosions in restive parts of the world. Indeed, even open warfare between great armies has been unable to stop the flow of oil for any appreciable time, even if such developments have propelled prices northward.

Perhaps no better example of destruction by weather exists than Hurricane Katrina, which in August 2005 devastated the Gulf

Coast. In the process, the unprecedented natural disaster crippled more than 25 percent of the nation's crude oil production and some 10–15 percent of America's refining. Major oil pipelines, from the Gulf region to the Midwest and the East Coast, were either shut down altogether or experienced critical capacity slowdowns. Two great pipelines were temporarily closed: the massive Colonial Pipeline that daily pumped more than 1.3 million barrels from the Gulf to the northeast, and the 1,400-mile Explorer Pipeline coursing from Louisiana to Texas and then up through the Midwest. With such a large drop in supply, prices spiked dramatically. Many service stations actually ran out of gasoline. Several major airports, including Washington's Dulles International, wondered if they could even obtain jet fuel. But international emergency measures increased the global oil supply, reduced consumption, and helped the United States weather the petroleum shortfall until the refineries and pipelines could be speedily repaired.[31] Despite even the wickedest winds and the highest seas, oil has continued to flow.

Industrial accidents from the minor to monumental have been a regular occurrence since the first gushers in 1859 in Pennsylvania, where commercial oil was born. The famous October 1927 Baba Gurgur strike in Iraq, the largest oil field for decades to come, erupted as a 90,000-barrel-per-day river of oil that raged unstoppable through the region for three days. Oil spills such as that of the *Exxon Valdez*, which spewed 10.8 million gallons into Alaska's Prince William Sound in March 1989, are famous but hardly the largest spill in recent years. In fact, during the two decades since, the world has witnessed 30 oil spills larger than the *Exxon Valdez*. During the 1990s, 346 spills occurred in excess of 2,000 gallons, or an average of about 10.6 million gallons annually—that is, an additional *Exxon Valdez* every year. The largest spill on record is from Pemex's Ixtoc I. From June 3, 1979, until it was capped 42 weeks later, Ixtoc I dumped an estimated 151.2 million gallons of crude into the Gulf of Mexico, most of which floated toward the Texas coastline.[32] Despite the most ruinous spills, oil has continued to flow.

Industrial accidents are equally common in the oil business. Oil rigs topple at sea, pipelines rust through, fires break out in the flammable world of petroleum and human error abounds. From the March 2001 explosions that killed ten people aboard the world's largest offshore oil platform, owned by Brazil's state oil firm Petrobras, to British Petroleum's August 2006 discovery that 16 of 22 miles of transit pipes serving the Trans-Alaska Pipeline were sufficiently corroded from neglect to warrant immediate replacement, the oil world is wracked with a ceaseless cavalcade of mishaps.[33] Despite the most worrisome damage and accompanying price spikes, repairs have always been mounted and oil has continued to flow.

Sabotage against the world's circulatory system for oil has been a fact of life since the inception of foreign oil. When the first commercial oil was drilled in Iran in 1908, local armed horsemen were hired as guards against the constant marauders attacking donkey trains laden with oil cans. Iraq's precious oil fields and pipelines were a regular target of local sabotage as part of the Arab jihad that began in the mid-twenties against colonial Great Britain. Local sabotage and terrorism as an oil industry phenomenon has never receded, only donned different insurgent monikers and masks. It never stops. In 2005, Ahwazi Arab insurgents dynamited numerous oil wells in Iranian Khuzestan, that nation's major oil center, thereby threatening some 10 percent of OPEC's production. Throughout 2006, the Movement for the Emancipation of the Niger Delta attacked Royal Dutch Shell's pipelines in Nigeria to bring that nation's oil to a standstill. In 2007, the Popular Revolutionary Army (EPR) launched a campaign of attacks against Pemex facilities in Mexico to topple the oil industry, this as an electoral protest. Off the coast of Somalia in early 2008, increasingly brazen pirates tried to hijack a Japanese oil tanker and might have except for the intervention of a German warship.[34] Despite a gamut of local explosions, attacks and subversions, oil has continued to flow.

Even open warfare has failed to choke off the world's supply. During World War II, Winston Churchill's experts devised complex but never implemented plans in "Operation Exporter" to destroy the entire Mideast oil infrastructure. The Allies were desperate to deny fuel to the Nazis in the wake of the Third Reich's alliance with the oil-rich Arab world. The Iran-Iraq War, in the 1980s, spawned the "Tanker War." During the conflict, Damascus had already blocked the pipeline over Syrian land that Iraq was using for access to the Mediterranean Sea and European oil markets. Some 9,000 Iraqi bombing runs were thrown against the Iran export facilities at Kharg Island. By 1984, the two combatant countries began attacking hundreds of oil tankers in the Persian Gulf, killing hundreds of innocent seamen. Armed Iranian speedboats set Iraqi vessels aflame, and Iraqi forces continuously retaliated in kind against Iranian and Kuwaiti ships. American and Russian maritime forces finally stepped in with their own flagged vessels as the war started to wind down. Years later, in 1991, Iraq's strongman Saddam Hussein set the Kuwait oil fields ablaze in a scorched earth campaign of unprecedented scale. A thousand Kuwaiti oil wells were ignited with thick smoke and flame so vast that astronomer Carl Sagan feared "a nuclear winter." Six million barrels were lost daily.[35] Despite the best efforts of some of the mightiest armies in history, oil has continued to flow.

But everything has changed, and changed for the worse.

TOPPLING THE HOUSE OF CARDS

In a situation that is worsening daily, oil supply resiliency has receded like the cartilage in a terribly weakened knee. Like any battered and bruised limb, the flexibility has simply been beaten out of global oil. The entire planet now teeters atop a slender cushion of a mere million barrels per day. Against this slim margin, the political will of key Mideast oil exporters such as Saudi Arabia to undertake surge production to make up for a shortfall is gone. Pivotal reserves such as Mexico's are rapidly dwindling as the world witnesses Pemex's annual double digit declines. Hyperventilating oil prices are continuously and permanently escalating in the face of a fast cheapening dollar. Anti-American alliances among numerous key OPEC countries, such as Venezuela and Iran, have now come together in stunning new coordination. Add the raging consumption of Asian countries such as India and China and the globe's house of oil cards is rattling—and rattling as never before. Should the tectonic forces of oil rub just wrong, the house will not only rattle, it could tumble.

How bad does it need to get to cripple the West's supply?

As of summer 2008, a mere 5 percent reduction in America's oil, or roughly about 1 million barrels per day, would be enough to trigger a release of oil from the Strategic Petroleum Reserve, subject to a presidential directive. That is the shortfall experienced in the aftermath of Hurricane Katrina when refineries were temporarily knocked offline. A 7 percent disruption would precipitate "an international crisis" under emergency treaties. More than 7 percent? Government experts in various countries who nervously monitor America's hour-to-hour oil supply have repeatedly stated that a 10 percent reduction in the U.S. supply—roughly two million barrels each day that cannot be found elsewhere—would be catastrophic. One key expert declared such a reduction would be "so off the chart that we cannot even model it."[36]

Weather and contained incidents of local sabotage and industrial disaster can still be temporarily absorbed. But some forms of coordinated international terrorism and concerted petropolitical manipulation simply cannot. Here the sole determinant is scale and the sustained level of disruption. How big? How long?

In two words, the apex of all oil terrorism targets is *Saudi Arabia*. The nation, which supplies more than 11 percent of all U.S. oil imports, does so through a string of three highly vulnerable choke points. It all begins in Saudi Arabia's broiling Eastern desert at the greatest petroleum repository in the world, the Ghawar Oil Field, so named for the noisome desert flies that populate this desolate clime. Ghawar is not the only oil field in Saudi Arabia, but it is the most productive and important—and indeed the most pivotal to the world's ability to function on a daily basis. From Ghawar, the rich Saudi ooze is piped to its first stop, the nearby Abqaiq processing facility operated by Saudi Arabia's Aramco Oil Company.[37]

At the wilderness Abqaiq facility, which processes two-thirds of all Saudi petroleum, the high-sulphur oil from Ghawar and other nearby fields is stabilized and otherwise prepared for seaborne export. From Abqaiq, the exportable crude is mainly piped to the nearby tank farm and port facility at Ras Tanura on the Persian Gulf. From this second point, the crude is loaded into an endless chain of thirsty supertankers.

To reach open seas, these supertankers must traverse the Persian Gulf and pass through the famous choke point at the Strait of Hormuz, the third and perhaps most perilous point of passage. This funnel waterway is not only the exit ramp for Saudi oil, but also for the enormous flows of Iranian and Iraqi crude. Some 18 million barrels per day traverse these waters.[38] Imagine a hand around a throat. Only then can one envision the strategic Strait of Hormuz.

Oft-cited without much detail, the Strait of Hormuz exists as a curvy channel some 21 miles wide following a hump-like course around the jutting thumb of peninsular Oman. The Strait's sometimes marshy, mainly shallow waters are deep enough for commercial traffic only in the middle, where two tanker-navigable shipping lanes have been established, one outbound and one inbound. Each lane in each direction is two miles wide. These twin two-mile lanes are separated by a two-mile buffer. Iranian missile installations and mountainous terrain pocked with endless potentially hostile caves and crannies directly overlook the Strait.[39]

The three choke points of Gulf Oil are nothing less than the solar plexus of the planet. Disabling any one of the three principal chokepoints—the Abqaiq processing plant, the Ras Tanura tanker facility, or the Strait of Hormuz—would immediately cripple world oil. International terrorism or Iranian retaliation could do it in mere hours. For a committed suicide killer or a doctrinaire state-sponsored attack, there is virtually no way to prevent such a catastrophe. Nearly every leading expert seems to agree that the question is not how or if, but when such a debacle would occur.

Al Qaeda has already probed the outer perimeters of Abqaiq in a February 2006 attack when two suicide bombers crashed their bomb-laden cars through the gates. Oil prices instantly jumped $2 per barrel. Although the attack was played down by Saudi officials as a mere fiery explosion with no impact, Department of Energy sources who monitor the minutia of Saudi oil security indicate that the attack was far more serious than has been publicized. One of the terrorist vehicles came perilously close to a critical Abqaiq installation, the source confirms.[40]

Certainly the Abqaiq camp, populated by some 30,000 mainly foreign workers, is protected by small armies of heavily armed security who will react first and ask questions second. However, what the Saudis fear most is not an attack by outside intruders, but rather an inside job orchestrated by infiltrated terrorists. That said, even if an insider blew up key facilities, oil engineers have stated that numerous redundant systems could speed a recovery.

The true nightmare scenario is an airborne attack, whether that be several hijacked airliners or a series of short-range missiles. Such an attack need not occur only once. It can be repeated again and again to decimate oil production for a protracted period. True, squadrons of Saudi jet fighters, such as F-15s, backed up by the complete resources of the Western military establishments, are always at the ready. But in truth, no F-15 can stop a hijacked 747—or several of them—hurtling toward the ground to destroy an installation. No dome of missile defense systems can intercept volleys of short-range missiles, which can reach their target within seconds.

Iran's regular military, as well as its independent 20,000-man Islamic Revolutionary Guard naval force and untold thousands of Al Kuds Special Forces, are equipped with an armada of speed boats, surface war vessels and submarines. The country's air force and land troops are highly trained, intensely maneuverable, implacably passionate and completely capable. Their history of sacrifice is legendary. Iranian troops raced to the front during the Iran-Iraq war carrying their own coffins, fervently eager to die in battle. Indeed, the country lost a generation of men in the process as scores of thousands died in a decade of futile war. Despite 21st century armies of hip, blue-jeaned, music-loving young people, Teheran still recruits legions of suicide bombers and other so-called martyrs in mass rallies held in sports arenas and other public venues.[41]

Iran's forces possess thousands of land-based, seaborne, and airborne missiles. Chinese Silkworm cruise missiles, French wave-hopping Exocet missiles, modified Russian Scuds and North Korean

No Dong and Taep'o Dong missiles renamed Shahabs 1 through 6 are in great abundance. They can be launched in conventional or unorthodox ways from land or sea, from truck or cave, from ship or sortie, stationary or mobile, day or night, guided by computer, satellite and the weight of a human finger.[42] These missiles cannot be completely stopped. Some could be, yes. But many would get through.

Islamic terrorist groups have access to some of the same weaponry as the Iranian military, especially Hezbollah, which is in fact an Iranian-sponsored terror group with ample coastal warfare experience. Many security experts also speak of a virtual shutdown of the Strait of Hormuz produced either by a credible threat against passage or token attacks. Maritime insurance could be suspended by a mere declaration of hostilities, that is, until nations guaranteed the war-risk. Others warn of a strategic sinking of a few tankers as being sufficient to block the slender bottleneck.[43]

If Ras Tanura or the Strait of Hormuz goes down, the Saudis can redirect oil to the East-West Petroline that traverses the Arabian Peninsula, terminating at the Red Sea. This reduced pipeline system can only accommodate a theoretical 5 million barrels daily, but as of the summer of 2008 only one-fifth that volume has actually moved through its 745-mile length. Moreover, five days would be added to the journey of a barrel of oil traveling to Asia. At the end of the day, the world's thirst for oil would be parched by 13 to 18 million barrels per day, depending upon the level and geographic diversity of destruction.[44]

The Strait of Hormuz, Ras Tanura and Abqaiq form nothing less than the Apocalyptic Triangle of modern civilization. A coordinated attack on any or all three of these would unleash Hell's beasts upon the Western world and bring it thudding to its knees.

DOLLAR WAR

But there is another way to choke off the West's supply of oil. It will not require missiles or hijacked airplanes but rather the ceaseless tintinnabulation of incremental OPEC price hikes in tandem with a concerted petroeconomic attack on America's dollar. Both campaigns are under way as of this writing.

The cost of a barrel rose almost daily throughout most of 2008. The price probably rose during the time it took to read this chapter. From May 2007 to May 2008, the price doubled from about $65 to about $130. Each day brings another record pointing north. Spiraling prices are not one-dimensional phenomena. They are driven by composite causes comprised of diverse regional and international strife, increased demand, rampant market speculation at the NYMEX trading center, and tight supply. But it is all a function of suppressed production. The oil industry since Rockefeller has manipulated supply, working hard to pump only enough oil to satisfy demand. A turn of the spigot to the left and the price goes up. A turn to the right and the flow becomes more plentiful, and prices soften.[45]

The infamous Mideast oil magnate Calouste S. Gulbenkian, the combative investor who owned 5 percent of all petroleum in Iraq and its adjacent regions, always bragged that oil was worth more in the ground than available on the market. If the system suffers, things are good. As oil becomes scarce, it becomes more valuable. Unlike most other commodities that yearn to be sold, oil interests reap wild profits as disruptions occur and the market is pressured. Record quarterly multibillion profits were predictably rung up by the main oil companies, surpassing the combined profitmaking of all other Fortune 500 companies combined. Exxon alone in February 2008 recorded a quarterly profit of 11.66 billion—that figure is not just income, but actual *profit*. Such billions amount to a profit level of $1,300 per second in 2007 for the one company. These stratospheric earnings leaped atop a cascade of continuous quarterly record profits. Aramco, the Saudi oil company, dwarfed American firms with 2006 revenues of more than $168 billion.[46]

The systematic transfer of American wealth and financial health to the Middle East and OPEC has been under way since the Yom Kippur War when the first Arab Oil Embargo was triggered. It began its 21st century climb immediately after the World Trade Center was attacked on September 11, 2001. Numbers that seemed mere threats and rhetoric at the end of 2007 have become dark inevitabilities. On November 17, 2007, Venezuelan president Hugo Chavez threatened to raise U.S. oil prices to $200 per barrel if Iran were attacked over her nuclear ambitions. That threat became moot. Six months later, the pundits were predicting $200 per barrel would be achieved within a year as matter of course.[47]

In February 2008, the Iranian Oil Bourse was opened to replace American currency alternatives such as the Yen and Euro. Iranian President Mahmoud Ahmadinejad declared the dollar was a "worthless piece of paper." The Bourse was part of a concerted strategy to wage economic war against the United States by virtue of devaluing the dollar and requiring more of it for oil.[48]

With rapid dollar devaluation, deliberate petrodollar exclusion and tornadic oil price escalation, a three-pronged economic warfare is under way. This is no secret. It is the stuff of the nightly news and page one. But to the amazement of history, Americans and the world are gladly driving toward their financial destiny in large, gas guzzling SUVs lulled by magnificent stereos, leather bucket seats and air conditioners on max. They stop along the way only for a car wash and espresso. The carmakers have made this procession not only unavoidable but seductive.

The oil stoppage may occur suddenly and ferociously as a result of a sustained terrorist disruption. Or it could be functionally stopped as a result of sustained slow motion economic attack wherein fuel will be available but so expensive that it will be unaffordable. Either way, fuel sufficiency can become both unattainable and the master of our fate.

The war to topple America at her exposed oil knee may begin with a bang. It may begin with a whimper.

CHAPTER THREE

A Thin Alliance

Operating out of a small, unimposing building in Paris, a short stroll from the Eiffel Tower, displaying a deceptively small plaque at the entrance, is an obscure organization that most people do not know exists but which is a prime focal point for every major policymaker and oil expert in the world. The offices belong to the International Energy Agency (IEA), known to the thousands who make it work and heed its communiqués, but unknown to the millions who may be dependent upon it for modern day survival. Some IEA staffers call their headquarters a "bunker." Indeed, some consider it a war room.[1]

Exactly what is the IEA?

The IEA is an intergovernmental, supranational body of 28 westernized countries established to ensure their uninterrupted global supply of oil and other energy. The members: Australia, Austria, Belgium, Canada, Czech Republic, Denmark, Finland, France, Germany, Greece, Hungary, Ireland, Italy, Japan, Republic of Korea, Luxembourg, The Netherlands, New Zealand, Norway, Poland, Portugal, Slovak Republic, Spain, Sweden, Switzerland, Turkey, United Kingdom and the United States. In addition, numerous non-member countries and international communities, such as the European Union, cooperate closely with the organization. The agency is, in fact, an adjunct to the Organization for Economic Cooperation and Development. Comprised of energy monitors, coordinators, statisticians, advisors and other petrocrats from government and industry, the IEA is prepared at a moment's notice to spring into action in the event of an oil shortage or stoppage.[2]

The IEA is hardly a secret. The agency publishes tall stacks of reports and studies that are disseminated to governmental agencies and industry analysts worldwide. It maintains an increasingly robust if serpentine website. But to the average person, the inner workings and protocols of the IEA are completely unknown. Most people don't even know the agency exists.

Invented after the 1973 Arab Oil Embargo, the IEA is quite simply designed to safeguard the industrialized world from an even greater petroleum calamity, whether caused by natural disaster, petropolitics, accident, war or terrorism. The IEA's unique powers to intervene in any domestic oil usage are endowed by international law and a 1974 multilateral treaty known as the Agreement on an International Energy Program (IEP) that pools the world's resources to ensure its common survival in our precarious oil age. Unknown to nearly all except the experts, the treaty's scope reaches into the garages of every household and the bus barns of every transit company, encompassing all vehicles, all forms of transportation, all supplies of energy and fuel and all storage and distribution.[3]

Exactly how the United States relates to the IEA in terms of its treaty obligations and expectations is the unseen dynamic that has the potential to make or break the nation's ability—or indeed the West's ability—to survive a sustained oil stoppage based upon hostile action.

The joint covenant of all IEA member nations is to help each other in the event a shortfall befalls any of them. In other words, if America's oil supply is interrupted for any reason, other IEA nations from France to New Zealand would be expected to help. Likewise, if France or New Zealand or any of the other member states experience an interruption, the United States would be obligated to help. America's membership in the IEA is both a reassurance and a burden since the notion of pooled resources cuts both ways and indeed all ways, just like any mutual defense treaty. Since the 28 nations of the IEA span four continents—from Japan and Korea in Asia, to France and Germany in Europe, to the Oceanic nations of Australia and New Zealand—the full spectrum of global threats looms large. Everything from an Asian cyclone to a Gulf hurricane, from Latin American sabotage to Mideast terrorism, could threaten supply and trigger the treaty.[4]

The single most important word in the IEA treaty and international relationship is "preparedness." IEA member nations must under international law be prepared, maintaining a strategic petroleum reserve sufficient for a 90-day supply that can be called upon in the event of a crisis. Due to the fungible nature of oil, world supply could be increased at any time by a mere local release. In other words, Spain could aid the United States by releasing its strategic stock in Madrid. New Zealand could do the same by releasing extra stockpiled oil in Auckland. With more oil in the system anywhere on the planet, prices stabilize and more supply becomes available.[5] That is the nature of fungible oil. If there is more to go around, more in fact will go around.

In the event that supplies were interrupted globally—say by a blockage of the Straits of Hormuz—numerous nations would have to join in a common effort to draw from their stockpiles. In such a case, it is unknown whether member countries would coordinate likeminded disciplined players in an orchestra or become a cacophonous assemblage of competitors, jealously hoarding their supplies and hedging their bets to protect their own national interests. Release of strategic reserves, called *stockdraw* in IEA parlance, is only one part of the IEA's coordinated program.

The second spear of the IEA's trident is *surge production*, that is, a temporary increase in supply by willing members.

Demand restraint is a third requirement and perhaps of greatest importance in a real crisis. Under IEA emergency demand restraint protocols, members must reduce immediate consumption by various methods—from simple marketing programs promoting carpools to alternative fuel switching programs, from emergency public transit procedures to outright partial or full bans on motor vehicles. The IEA categorizes its demand restraint protocols along three levels with telling names: "light-handed measures," "medium-handed measures" and "heavy-handed measures." So-called light-handed measures include such actions as ride-sharing advertising campaigns. Medium- to heavy-handed efforts include a range of actions from mandatory speed reduction and parking restrictions to vehicle use prohibitions, such as driverless days.[6]

Certainly, the IEA has shown its ability to step in temporarily to help alleviate a temporary shortage. On August 29, 2006, Hurricane Katrina crippled key American pipelines and refining, causing gas stations to run dry and prices to soar. Within a week, IEA member countries announced that the equivalent of 60 million barrels would be added to the world's supply. A multilateral effort employed all three methods: demand restraint, surge production and stockdraw, either by taking from strategic reserves or the equivalent by reducing reserve requirements. Some 87 percent of that temporary extra world supply was achieved by an international strategic release or reduction of reserves. Surge production amounted to 11 percent. Just 2 percent resulted from demand restraint. With that international assistance, America was given the breathing space to quickly repair the damage to its refining and pipeline distribution, enduring a minimum of economic and supply chaos.[7]

At first glance, the IEA treaty seems like a perfect system of safeguards. However, a closer look is far less reassuring. Indeed, like much of Washington's oil policy, America's relationship to the IEA points up not the strengths, but the vulnerabilities.

True, the IEA is willing to act in the event of any local emergency, such as damage to South Korean oil lines by North Korean war action should that occur, or a Japanese earthquake, or a Hurricane Katrina in the U.S. But it is true that mandated powers are not triggered until a global shortage occurs amounting to 7 percent of the worldwide usage. At press time, the world consumes some 86 million barrels per day, so the triggering shortfall would amount to about 5.8 million barrels per day in global supply. At that point, the IEA can invoke its treaty powers to "require" voluntary compliance with coordinated action along all three emergency vectors: demand restraint, surge production, and strategic stockdraw. The key tenet is the anachronistic requirement for "voluntary domestic action" in concert with other countries. Compliance can be *required* but not *compelled*. Hence, the 28-nation IEA can become an inert apparatus by the action or inaction of a single nation.[8]

A subcutaneous examination reveals the details of America's vulnerability even as it enjoys the seeming protection of an international force for oil stability.

Start with the reserve. A cornerstone of the IEA's treaty requires all nations to maintain a 90-day strategic petroleum reserve. America does not. The U.S, as of summer 2008, maintains a mere 58-day supply of net imports. The treaty requirement is circumvented through a loophole engineered for the United States allowing Washington to count commercial holdings in local tanks and even the functionally inaccessible contents stuck in the long lengths of pipelines traversing the country.[9]

MANAGING STRATEGIC SUPPLIES

Actually, America maintains three separate strategic oil reserves. The most important is the much-heralded Strategic Petroleum Reserve (SPR) deposited in four massive salt caverns along the Gulf Coast. Its inventory grows incrementally, siphoning off a mere tenth of a percent of the world's supply each day. This miniscule accretion avoids any appreciable effect on global demand. The source is mainly but not exclusively "in-kind" trades with domestic oil companies that lease federal oil lands and pay their leases with oil instead of money.[10]

Together, the various deep salt caverns can hold 727 million barrels, all unrefined crude oil. The contents are useless without refining capability. Hence, in the event refineries are disabled, as they were during Hurricane Katrina, the country could have brimming oil at the ready, but no refined gasoline to fuel trucks and cars.[11]

Full storage levels have almost been reached, and the government has sought legislation to double capacity by adding additional caverns. Once the White House authorizes any SPR release, it takes about 13 days for stored stocks to flow into the nation's oil veins and capillaries. The 58-day presumed supply is enough to help the nation operate normally during a crisis. How much is that? The nation might lack 5 million barrels per day because of a Hormuz-region shutdown. Or a joint knockout of American facilities and Saudi supply lines could produce a devastating 10 million barrels per day shortfall. But any volume of oil can be released daily, depending upon presidential discretion. At full throttle, the SPR can release as much as 4.2 million barrels per day. But after a period of time, the emptying process reduces the flow pressure, and the maximum flow rate would reduce to about half that level. Planners know that by reducing the flow to a mere 1 million barrels daily, approximating the level necessitated by the Katrina disaster—that is, about 5 percent—the existing 58-day reserve can be stretched many more months. But then if too little is released, the reserve will leave many gas tanks wanting.[12]

The SPR is stop-gap. To be effective, the release volume would need to be commensurate with shortfall. Any severe shutdown extending more than two months would functionally drain the SPR.

A second and far more obscure stockpile, the Northeast Home Heating Oil Reserve, maintains approximately two million barrels of emergency reserve stored in New Jersey and Connecticut. The contents are home heating oil only. The 2 million barrels are enough for about a week or two of assistance in the event of a wintertime supply problem for the 5.3 million northeast corridor families that still heat their homes with oil.[13] In any protracted crisis, this reserve would not last through the first two or three winter weekends.

Even less known is the third reserve, the Naval Petroleum and Oil Shale Reserves. The so-called "Naval Petroleum Reserve" is not an assemblage of ready to pump tank farms or storage caverns but rather a network of rich shale fields that can be utilized for domestic production in an emergency. Under long-controversial federal charters, those fields are now being commercially exploited by major oil companies.[14] They are essentially no longer functioning as a reserve, but are part of the nation's domestic production.

Although most people believe the concept of an SPR was born

after the first 1973 Arab Oil Embargo, in fact, most 20th century presidents advocated the concept long before that.

The idea began at the end of the 19th century when Washington considered strategic stockpiles of certain vital minerals and commodities. Oil was not specified back then because it was not yet the pivotal war commodity it would soon become. The idea of an actual petroleum reserve was first proposed during the run-up to World War I as the U.S. Navy switched from slow refueling coal-burning warships to fast oil-burning vessels. In 1910, the Pickett Act authorized President William Taft to set aside petroleum producing lands —including the infamous "Teapot Dome" tract in Wyoming, so named for a rotunda-like rocky prominence. Teapot Dome created a valued emergency oil source in the event of war. However, the next president, Warren G. Harding, saw his legacy brought down by the oil company leasing scandal surrounding the Teapot Dome reserve. Ultimately, four tracts in California, Wyoming, Utah and Alaska became collectively known as "the Naval Petroleum Reserve," ready for exploitation in a crisis. In 1942, during World War II, President Franklin Delano Roosevelt expanded the available oil-producing lands within the Naval Petroleum Reserve. But still, no ready storage had been established.[15]

Two years later, in 1944, FDR's Secretary of the Interior, Harold Ickes, proposed a formal strategic reserve filled with immediately usable crude. At the time, the Nazis had forged an alliance with Arab oil-exporting states and the international Arab Higher Committee. The Allies rightly feared their access to Iraqi and Mideast oil would soon disappear with supplies to the Reich flowing in abundance. Winston Churchill expressed the fear that the Third Reich could win the war on the basis of oil unless the Arab-Nazi oil alliance was disrupted by a broad campaign of military sabotage. A campaign to completely destroy the Mideast oil infrastructure in 1941 was never launched. The heroic "Operation Exporter" succeeded at the last minute, checking Nazi influence on Mideast production and distribution lines by a combination of clandestine efforts in Lebanon and local military routs in Iraq. Even though the Arab-Nazi Alliance—in large measure engineered by the Mufti of Jerusalem--was fractured, the Allies remained concerned right through the end of the conflict. Still no oil reserve per se was created during the war.[16]

In 1952, during the Korean War, President Harry Truman's Minerals Policy Commission once again resurrected the idea of a strategic oil store. President Dwight D. Eisenhower also suggested an oil reserve after the 1956 Suez Crisis. His successor, President Richard Nixon in 1970 similarly encouraged the creation of a reserve.[17]

Not until the Arab Oil Embargo of 1973 did Congress and President Gerald Ford finalize the decades-long desire to maintain a ready stockpile by creating the Strategic Petroleum Reserve.[18] But this has proved to be only a short-term, time-buying device that has been totally outmoded by the world's insatiable demand for oil, the decay of the supply cushion, and new strategies for long-term disruption that have exceeded the direst consequence of conventional warfare.

THE URGE TO SURGE

The second plank of the IEA's plan for survival involves surge production. This concept certainly made sense during the first decades of the IEA in the last century, when excess capacity existed and cooperative production partners would help out. But the likelihood of surge production is now little more than fumes.

Like the secretive Hostmen of 16th and 17th century England, and the corrupt Rockefeller-Flagler combine of 19th century America, and the Red Line monopolists of the mid–20th century, OPEC and other oil producers have learned to produce only enough fuel to barely satisfy a thirsty market. The steady transfer of American and Western wealth to the Middle East has been under way since the Oil Shock of October 1973 when the Arabs punished the U.S. and Europe for supporting Israel. This transfer received a jolting northward boost just months after the attacks of September 11 when OPEC production was artificially reduced to ignite higher prices. Oil essentially doubled from $25 to $50 per barrel from 2004 to 2005. It doubled again from $63 in 2007 to 2008. In early 2008, after breaching the psychological barrier of $100 per barrel, $5 and $6 per week price hikes became commonplace.[19] As this chapter is being written, new record prices are being announced daily.

In truth, OPEC won't pump an extra gallon if it means slowing the constant upward spiral of global prices. This sad fact was stunningly made apparent to the world when in January 2008 President George W. Bush visited Saudi Arabia, many said "hat in hand." Bush's mission was to ask Saudi royalty to soften oil prices for the good of the fuel-battered American economy. Stinging increases began eroding American economic strength and became a major contribution to the 2008 recession.[20]

In response to Bush's plea for more production and fewer price spikes, Saudi Oil Minister Ali al-Nuaimi curtly refused. With the world media listening, al-Nuaimi replied, "We will raise production when the market justifies it." Headlines globally reported the stultifying response as the unsympathetic anti-Western rebuff that it was.[21] The West had been put on notice like never before: The only thing that could surge was prices.

The scene was repeated in May 2008 when Bush again visited and beseeched Saudi royalty for more production. Spurned a second time, the President after resisting the demands of Congress, immediately ordered the SPR to stop adding new inventory. Because the SPR accrues at so infinitesimal a level, the move was immediately declared by experts to be exactly what it was: a droplet in a pipeline.[22]

LACK OF RESTRAINT

The most important part of any IEA rescue plan during an oil crisis is the most obvious: *demand restraint.* Nothing reduces the problem of an oil shortage more than a plan to reduce actual consumption.

New Zealand has a plan. Its International Energy Agreement Act of 1976 supplemented by its Petroleum Demand Restraint Act 1981 gives the New Zealand government the power to take over and direct petroleum distribution, the power to ban vehicles, and the right to implement other emergency measures to reduce demand.[23]

The Czech Republic has a plan. That country in 1999 passed its Emergency Oil Stocks Act, which provides for restrictions and even outright bans on all forms of oil consumption, including aviation fuel. Speed reduction, odd-even license plate bans, gas station closures, and prohibitions on selling gasoline in private containers are among the many measures actually recited in the legislation. Its plan also specifies emergency committees and coordination as the country draws down on its stockpile. The Czech Republic's law has been updated from time to time since enactment.[24]

Poland has a plan. Newly admitted into the IEA, the sweeping emergency oil crisis legislation Poland enacted in 2007 permits the banning or restriction of any motor vehicle or marine vessel, and even allows federal cancellation of events in which motor vehicles or vessels are used, such as car races and speedboat displays.[25]

Japan has a plan. The country has enacted several emergency laws and regulations: The Petroleum Supply and Demand Optimization Law and the Emergency Law for Stabilization of National Life both enable Tokyo to restrict any modality of oil consumption during a fuel crisis.[26]

In country after country, tried, tested, studied and successful demand restraint measures—vehicle restrictions and odd-even bans, fuel switching, retrofitting, and public transit increases—are ready to roll out. The United States has no such plan. Washington's plan is to release some oil from the Strategic Oil Reserve until it may run out. But then, the plan is simply to spend more, according to Washington officials repeatedly questioned. The plan is to allow "market forces" to control the situation, they insist. In that scenario, everyone in the country and consequently nearly everyone else in the fungible world, will pay more, spend more, struggle more, deplete more.

Along the lines of buying our way out of a critical crisis, Washington actually plans in a desperate moment to economically hijack a tanker at sea for emergency oil. "Commonly oil tankers do not know where the ultimate or final destination until they hit the ocean," explains one key government energy official, "and not infrequently are re-routed on the high seas, depending upon the price paid. If someone gets outbidded, those tankers are rerouted. The rich nations can outbid the poor ones."[27]

Another Washington energy official adds, "We can outbid anyone, China, India. We will get that tanker. This nation does not have a demand restraint program. Period. Our plan is to buy our way out of any crisis."[28]

Dollar and oil demand are on a mid-air collision course long visible on the world's radar. Oil shipment destinations and even pipeline flows are increasingly pre-contracted—as they are between Venezuela and China, as they will be soon along the Sarnia Line #9 to Eastern Canada—and cannot be diverted. Plans to elevate pinprick pipe demolitions to protracted infrastructure mega-disruptions are tediously planned by people in tents using candlelight and inauspicious low-rent apartments connected to terror networks far away by disposable cell phones. The world is entering an era where dollar warfare is in fact the petropolitical weapon of choice. In such a roiling world, America's secret weapon for surviving an extended physical or economic stoppage cannot be deeper and deeper pockets. It needs a real plan.

Such a plan will hurt. It will anger. But when the fever breaks, the country will be cured—forever.

CHAPTER FOUR

Week One— The Shock and the First Restrictions

On first reading, *The Plan's* specifics will seem intolerable to the many individuals inconvenienced and sidelined by its temporary restrictive provisions. But surely the entire nation has known since the Oil Shock of 1973 that a crisis day was coming for petroleum. Despite omnipresent tobacco-style warnings of oil vulnerability, Detroit designed and manufactured ever larger and thirstier gas guzzlers, which were sexed up and marketed by Madison Avenue, then enthusiastically purchased, financed, and ostentatiously operated on Main Street in every city. If *The Plan* must go into effect, it only means that the day of reckoning has arrived. That crisis day will bring the true protracted oil emergency that shall necessitate aggressive measures to keep the nation mobile, minimize the effects of petroleum warfare and shepherd the world away from an oil addiction future.

Or, perhaps, a finally savvy, oil-battered society will see the great inevitable debacle looming so close that it elects to implement *The*

Plan before the disaster strikes. This option is the true goal of this work. Don't wait. Move against the crisis before the crisis moves against us.

Either way, *The Plan* manifests as a series of temporary "regulations" designed to ration and organize limited oil supplies, prioritize usage, and then effectuate a true fix. These rules are just the beginning backbone of restoring the nation to energy health. Many more regulations, enforcement procedures, and fine points will be needed to close loopholes and make the proposal more effective.

Under scrutiny, *The Plan* treats a protracted oil crisis as any responsible government would treat a weather catastrophe, great snowstorm, water drought, electricity shortfall, heat emergency or other grave natural disaster. Its proposed mandates carefully draw on existing but neglected international treaty obligations, programs and guidelines, as well as existing oil crisis legislation in other westernized nations. Those programs have been combined with our own 20th century American wartime history and the record of this nation's countless local and regional emergencies. All this precedent and protocol is then fused together by common sense and clear thinking to create *The Plan* that follows.

The Plan uses existing inter-governmental standards for declaring an emergency. An oil supply emergency would be triggered by a protracted 5 to 10 percent shortfall in petroleum. "Protracted" is a period longer than thirty days.

If society waits until the disruption dictates the moment, the transition will indeed be painful. But if *The Plan* is implemented before an emergency, the transition can be far more tolerable, and measurably less painful.

Either way, few will be happy at first. But only a nation going cold turkey will eventually kick the addiction. Either way, if done properly, and if accompanied by the immediate retrofit called for—itself a daunting challenge, the discomfort of *The Plan* should be brief and survivable. Here is *The Plan*.

Regulation 1: Price Stabilization and Roll Back. Within 24 hours of an oil supply emergency declaration, the wholesale price of all oil produced in the US will be rolled back to the price existing on January 1, 2006.

DISCUSSION

The very first act of managing an oil supply emergency should be aimed at the pump price of oil. Obviously, the cost at the pump is only the "final price" per gallon. Society expends an estimated $14 to $35 per gallon for such externalized costs as military defense, environmental damage and related health expense.[1]

Although externalized prices affect society and taxpayers at large, pump prices hit the individual immediately and most visibly. Many will be hit very hard during any price escalation crisis. More than a few will be unable to afford the gas needed to conduct their lives. Some will be unable to purchase the gas needed to even save their lives.

Knee-jerk logic asserts that the market forces of supply and demand should dictate the price per gallon. By this thinking, as gasoline becomes more scarce for any reason, the price should soar. But in truth, oil pricing does not abide by the rules of free market capitalism—and never has.

Since the beginning of recorded history, fuel has always been the domain of monarchists, monopolists and manipulators. It began thousands of years ago with wood as civilization's first fuel. Wood was the ancient fuel behind smelting, the process for the metal-making required to create weapons, tools, jewelry, coins and the other basics of civilization. Indeed, wood was more valuable than gold. Why? Because without wood, there was no gold. As the most precious commodity on earth, it is no wonder that in ancient times, pharaohs, kings and emperors controlled the market and distribution of all wood.[2]

When an early 17th century timber shortage forced England into the world's first fuel crisis, western civilization switched to the first alternative fuel: coal. It was a dirty, polluting and deadly alternative, but it was all a rapidly industrializing society could turn to. In those years, England's supply of coal was shrewdly manipulated by a secret society known as the Hostmen of Newcastle—the first fuel cartel. Reviled for their corruption and political control, the Hostmen mined and transported just enough coal to maintain high prices. The pattern of market manipulation invented by the Hostmen never stopped. Their example continued centuries after they disappeared, becoming emblematic of the fuel industries to come.[3]

Indeed, western oil itself was born and raised outside the realm of free market capitalism. When in 1858 petroleum was first commercially drilled in Pennsylvania, it did not take long for the Rockefellers and Flaglers, operating through Standard Oil, to turn the manipulation of oil supplies into a well-honed criminal enterprise. Too much oil would cause a glut. Curtailing supply in the face of growing demand would create a bonanza. So Rockefeller and Flagler cunningly adjusted their drilling, refining and distribution accordingly, playing society like a violin. Their widespread use of corporate fraud, masked subsidiaries and market deceit in the late 1800s provoked the well-known and oft-used antitrust and antimonopoly laws in place today.[4]

Later, France and England developed an oil industry during the first decades of the 20th century—not by virtue of free enterprise, but through exploitative government-financed and supported western imperialism. In the post–World War I oil frenzy of the 1920s, England deployed two quasi-governmental commercial oil arms, British Petroleum and London's reinvented Royal Dutch, to monopolize Mesopotamian oil even before the region's first gusher. At the same time, France used an amalgam of government-controlled companies that eventually became known as Total to join the British in colonizing and parceling up Mesopotamian oil. Their manipulated oil concessions became enshrined as international law under cover of the League of Nations, which rewarded the French and British with oil for their victorious roles in the war against Germany and Turkey.[5]

Turkey owned the Mideast oil lands until the League awarded them to the Allies. America insisted on joining the Anglo-French monopoly, even though the U.S. was not a member of the League of Nations. Thus European and American oil imperialism in the

Mideast was crowned in 1924 by the League of Nations as official spoils of World War I. In the process, a new oil state was created, the nation of "Iraq." That is how America, Britain and France became entrenched in Iraq. They came not as conquerors but as oil imperialists—and at first they were indeed triumphant.[6]

Yet in reality, western oil concerns established their footing in the oil-rich Mideast as government vanguards, not free marketers. Nor did they pursue any course other than market manipulation once they became established. Oil companies quickly adjusted supply to keep demand prices up. Calouste Sarkis Gulbenkian, the 20th century Armenian oil magnate known as "Mr. Five Percent," comprehended the process completely from the beginning. Gulbenkian earned his nickname for his 5 percent control of the 1928 "Red Line Agreement" that monopolized Middle East oil for Britain, France and America. In essence, although an individual, Gulbenkian was a full partner in Mideast oil with the governments of France, England and the United States. As such, Gulbenkian was fully qualified to periodically sneer to his partners that he understood the truth about their market ploys. The longer oil stayed in the ground, he asserted, the more valuable it became.[7]

During the decades after World War II, Gulbenkian's Red Line Agreement morphed and metastasized into the 21st century Mideast oil cartels that we know today.[8]

Creation of the western oil companies in the Middle East by European and American government action was only the beginning. Sustaining those oil companies required continuous and uninterrupted multibillion dollar annual military, economic and industrial support, without which the supply lines could never be maintained or protected. Oil is the only commodity America and its allies import that is protected by an extraordinarily costly global military presence.[9] Neither crucial copper nor vital platinum enjoys that sort of protection—not even diamonds do.

Hence, other precious resource companies, energy developers, and general corporate investors from Google to General Electric must suffer the free market risks and costs of overseas operations, but oil tycoons can rely upon taxpayer-supported militaries. Thus, the oil business is not a free market enterprise. Its legacy is one of government imperialism. Its development is based on market manipulation. Its continuation is official government policy—not the vagaries of the free marketplace.

After decades of exploitation, the tables have now turned, and it is the oil nations that have the West over a barrel. Today the industrialized world is in the grip of the oil exporters, a grip that is squeezable at will. Oil in our century—who owns it and who controls it—has evolved from a mere monopolistic enterprise designed to make men wealthy into a petropolitical, anti-western weapon designed to conduct creeping economic warfare and topple societies in the ongoing clash of civilizations.

Oil exporters now have the ability to cavalierly amass great fortunes at our expense. Saudi Arabia could purchase Bank of America with one month's profit. Entire national economies can be crippled and strategic might disabled—in fact, the very viability of the western society that the exporters so detest can be unraveled—all with a mere turn of the spigot.[10] Indeed, when the valve is nudged even slightly to the left, America instantly feels the choking sensation.

Saudi princes aver before television cameras that oil prices are the product of a free-spirited, world-wide market that spans the globe. Yet we see carve-outs and price controls at will. Exporter governments maintain gasoline cheap and plentiful for their own drivers. As of summer 2008, Saudi Arabia sold gasoline at 91 cents per gallon, Kuwait at 78 cents per gallon, Nigeria at 38 cents per gallon, and Venezuela's gas stations filled customer vehicles at 12 cents per gallon.[11] Applying the doctrine of fungibility and global "supply and demand," that means that drivers throughout the western and non-exporting world are subsidizing citizens of those oil-rich nations.

In truth, fuel prices are constantly manipulated by governments. They are subsidized, rolled back and inflated and deflated at will. Venezuelan president Hugo Chavez threatened to instantly double the price of oil to $200 per barrel if the United States, either unilaterally or in defense of Israel, attacked Iran as part of the escalating stand-off with Tehran over its nuclear ambitions.[12] That was not the free market talking. That was a threat to price oil as an economic weapon. Ironically, Chavez's threat became an apparent inevitability as petroleum then quickly soared to almost $150 per barrel.

To be certain, there is nothing about the oil business—except the desire for tornadic profits—that conforms to the commonly accepted principles of free enterprise or free market capitalism. The entire system is controlled to squeeze and manipulate both commercial and individual consumers worldwide. To avoid the specter of an imposed oil shortage creating a crisis gasoline market that only the most affluent and ostentatious gas guzzlers can afford and average citizens cannot, the price of oil must be stabilized, frozen or indeed rolled back. If oil cannot be imported at the rolled back price, domestic supplies should be controlled at the rollback price. Indeed, the substantial reduction of the American market for escalating imported oil will flatten global prices. America accounts for approximately 25 percent of global petroleum usage.[13]

January 1, 2006, which predates the most virulent spirals of post-September 11 era, seems an equitable rollback point. Without price stability, the nation will devolve into price gouging and supply hoarding. Mobility itself will be reserved for the well-to-do, creating class warfare in transportation wherein some people will be unable to get to work or the hospital while others can cruise along Sunset Strip or Ocean Drive in their Navigators and Escalades to attend parties. In that case, the oil weapon will begin taking immediate social casualties. America will have lost before its adversaries can win. Nor will price rollbacks discourage conservation. In tandem with other regulations temporarily restricting automobiles on the basis of MPG until they are retrofitted to flex-fuel or alt fuel, price rollbacks will merely ease the pain. Gasoline will still be in short supply—just more affordable.

Price rollbacks are, of course, common. The United States and nations everywhere have used them throughout recent history to cure inappropriate escalation in price hikes, price gouging, windfall profit, market inequities or price rigging. The spectrum of price-controlled and rolled-back items in recent commercial history ranges from mortgages and merchandise to meat and milk, from credit card fees and cargo costs to electricity usage and oil at the pump. Indeed, rollbacks commonly occur every time a natural disaster strikes whenever price gouging laws are applied.[14]

In an emergency, there is little that America can do to roll back world oil prices. However, America can control the price of oil produced here. And it should. Rolling back the domestic price of oil to the 2006 average of about $58 per barrel will only bring the price of gasoline at the pump down by a hoped for 30 to 40 percent because oil prices are set by a global market. That could only be a moderating factor in a true emergency as prices will certainly multiply. Indeed, restoring the 2006 domestic price will still contribute to an economic hardship for many, for sure. Gasoline prices during 2006 zigzagged under $3 per gallon. That 2006 level is still double the price paid in 2001. But such a rollback will approximately halve the price prevailing during the domestic summer of 2008. More than that, the price will stabilize further as America substantially transitions off oil once and for all. Most importantly, American oil companies and supply will not become a partner in nor benefit from the economic assault against the public any crisis is expected to inflict.

> **Regulation 2: SPR Release and Cessation of Resupply.** During the oil supply emergency, the Strategic Petroleum Reserve shall be drawn down until exhaustion to help offset any shortfall in necessary imported oil. The reserve shall not be refilled during the emergency.

DISCUSSION

The Strategic Petroleum Reserve (SPR) is a mere stopgap resource, storing approximately two months' worth of imported crude, longer if the release flow volume is lessened. The SPR cannot solve any protracted problem. It can only buy the country time—a very short period of time.

Two separate dynamics are at play, especially when the SPR is considered in tandem with similar allied storage facilities in other countries such as Korea and Poland. The first is *price*. The second is *availability* at any price.

By releasing America's SPR, the spike in prices is alleviated because supply will be increased. If International Energy Agency (IEA) allies do the same within their respective countries, that will create a broad international downward pressure on the cost of a barrel. However, moving reserves from Korea, Poland and other IEA nations into America's gas tanks is a separate logistical question involving oceans and enormous additional cost. It is fundamentally impractical. Moreover, in the event of a terrorism-invoked interruption, the crisis will be worldwide. Other nations may be pressured by their own populations to not share. Or, allied nations may be blackmailed away from assistance. International commercial maritime resupply has traditionally been targeted in warfare.

Thus, if the SPR is designed to "buy time," the purchase of those eight weeks should be to implement an operational plan of demand restraint and simultaneous retrofitting to flex-fuel and alt fuel. It must all be implemented at breakneck speed even though the eight weeks in question will be barely a beginning. Naturally, if the SPR is releasing oil, acquisition of new crude inventories shall be suspended. Suspension of acquisition offers a negligible effect on market prices, even though such a stoppage was authorized by Washington as an election year political gimmick in 2008. The level of acquisition is just a fraction of a percent daily. In the end, getting off oil will lead to doing away with the stopgap SPR altogether.

Regulation 3: Shortages. In an oil supply emergency, emergency management shall take control of supply and distribution, allotting petroleum as needed while recognizing priorities for emergency, military, and governmental users, as well as those rendering critical services such as health services. Anti-hoarding measures shall be implemented, including but not limited to prohibitions against filling individual containers or other storage vessels designed to resell or hoard petroleum products. Gasoline shall only be dispensed into original factory vehicle fuel tanks. It shall be a felony to sell, resell, distribute, redistribute or transfer petroleum outside pre-existing, licensed supply and retail channels, except by a licensed emergency road repair vehicle. Violators who receive or transfer petroleum will be subject to prosecution and vehicle seizure.

DISCUSSION

Price controls automatically invoke fear of shortages and rightly so. The last time windfall taxes and price controls were imposed upon the oil industry, in the early 1980s, shortages resulted. Modern bureaucrats have proven that they possess an uncanny ability to make well-intentioned controls insufferable to all.[15]

But sometimes controls are necessary over a short-term. Most allies in the IEA have provisions for exercising temporary control of oil production and distribution in the event of an oil emergency. Such powers are written right into the legislation of such IEA nations as Poland, New Zealand and Czechoslovakia.[16]

Moreover, America's own wartime history involved strict control of many raw materials, including oil. Those regulations helped the country prevail. For example, in 1942, FDR issued Executive Order 9276 creating the Petroleum Administration for War. This sweeping order governed all aspects of oil production, distribution and rationing. The Petroleum Administrator could allocate how much oil would flow, where, and under what circumstances. America was divided into five so-called Petroleum Administration Defense Districts or PADDs. PADD1 encompassed the East Coast, PADD2 represented the Midwest, PADD3 stretched across the Gulf Coast and adjacent regions, PADD4 was the Rocky Mountain Empire and PADD5 bureaucratically grouped California and the Pacific Northwest with Hawaii and Alaska.[17]

The Petroleum Administration for War was abolished after World War II but was resurrected during the Korean War in a different form by the Defense Production Act of 1950. After the Korean War, the office again went out of business, with its energy oversight duties absorbed by the Department of Interior. However, the original PADD system remains in place today as the Department of Energy's main approach to day-to-day tracking serving as framework for the regional demand and distribution of petroleum. In fact, the five PADDs are still prominently mapped on the department's website and burned into the department's tradition. PADDs are ready at any time to roll back into their original purpose, allowing the government to manage oil supplies region-by-region, especially since those regions have different seasonal needs. That said, without new enabling regulations, the PADDs today remain mere statistical conveniences.[18]

To be sure, state and federal governments possess considerable experience regulating consumer prices for utilities such as electricity, gas, water and telephone. What's more, many nations have long controlled their oil industries as nationally owned or quasi-national enterprises. In recent years, American oil has been exempt from the type of public regulation or ownership imposed upon other energy industries such as natural gas and electricity, even though the oil industry thrives and exists as a dependent byproduct of Washington's military-industrial complex.

For example, oil receives multibillion dollar annual subsidies in spite of its cyclonic profits. America's military defends the supply lines at great peril. The nation's vast diplomatic powers are at oil's disposal. Certainly, the end-use for the bulk of oil, the transportation sector, completely depends upon a government financed and maintained infrastructure. Specifically, the government owns all the roads and highway system. Hence, in an emergency—or to forefend one—Washington has ample basis upon which to resurrect strict oil distribution control. This would involve close public utility–style oversight of the corporate oil infrastructure if necessary, just as is typically enabled in the legislation of other countries and has occurred in America during its various 20th century wars.

Guarding against shortages will involve more than taking official control of the massive oil supply most visible to all at the pumps. It will also involve the kinds of anti-hoarding measures typically invoked after natural disasters. These measures will apply to individuals and groups attempting to circumvent the emergency system. Such standard rules as no topping off, fuel rationing, a coupon program, prohibitions against gas stations filling portable containers, and strict measures to keep a black or gray market at bay will become instantly necessary. Siphoning between cars, or dispensing from any source not part of the existing channel or the roadside emergency network, will also be prohibited. Security will become a major issue as vehicles will undoubtedly be carjacked not for their stereos or plush interiors but the gasoline sloshing in the tank.

> **Regulation 4: Price Gouging.** It shall be a felony to exceed the stabilized price for petroleum products. Anti-price gouging measures shall be implemented, including prominent notices posted at all pumps and dispensing locations; these notices shall include toll-free numbers, a government enforcement website and email address to report violations. Misprision of such violations or other failure to report such violations by any individual shall be a prosecutable offense under 18 U.S.C. § 4 or other applicable statutes.

DISCUSSION

Vigilance against price gouging is a feature of many natural disasters and emergencies, from snowstorms to hurricanes. Indeed, oil in such emergencies is an established focus of anti-price gouging enforcement. The Department of Energy and numerous local and state jurisdictions acted during Hurricane Katrina to guard against price gougers at the pump.[19]

As of summer 2008, the department's website still devotes a full section to the topic with the admonition: "The Department of Energy is very concerned about the impact of gasoline prices on American families. While we are working to address longer term supply issues, we're also working to make sure American families are being treated fairly. If you believe there may be price gouging or price fixing, please contact your local authorities." The DOE website includes a complaint form and toll-free number. A stern declaration warns: "All complaints registered with the Department of Energy will be collated and transmitted to the Federal Trade Commission, U.S. Department of Justice, and individual State Attorneys General for investigation and prosecution where appropriate."[20]

Stamping out price gouging as well as the black or gray market is imperative if oil is to be truly stabilized. This will allow the country to get back on its feet economically and tactically in the midst of an oil emergency.

> **Regulation 5: MPG Restrictions.** Within 48 hours of an oil supply emergency being declared, all non-commercial passenger vehicles registered in an extended metropolitan urban setting that are EPA-rated less than 15 MPG will be permanently grounded until retrofitted for flex-fuel or alt fuel. Until retrofitted for flex fuel or alt fuel, all non-commercial passenger vehicles registered in a metropolitan urban setting that are EPA-rated from 16-25 MPG will be allowed to run on a once-per-week schedule, with the allowable day of the week determined by the last digit or letter of their license plate unless an alternate date is applied for; and those EPA-rated from 26-35 MPG will be allowed to operate on an every-other-day schedule with the allowable day of the week determined by the last digit or letter of their license plate, unless an alternate date is applied for. All non-commercial passenger vehicles rated 36 MPG or higher will be unrestricted on condition these vehicles are also scheduled for retrofitting for flex-fuel or alt fuel within twelve months. This rule is to be enforced by state motor vehicle agencies, which can issue a non-transferable multi-day per week permit once per month to facilitate special intrastate or interstate driving plans or genuine hardship exemptions.

DISCUSSION

In the first week of an oil supply emergency, all jurisdictions will have to act *instantly* to restrict consumption. The same approach is commonly used in a water shortage. This is the demand restraint inherent in IEA protocols and the "power ingredient" in the legislation of other IEA countries. Even when oil emergencies are not declared, alternate day driving restrictions are common in many countries during both peacetime and war to cope with scarce or expensive fuel supply. Center city driving bans or restrictions have been successfully imposed in London to alleviate congestion. China declared every other day driving to improve air quality for the Olympics. HOV lanes, that is, High Occupancy Vehicle lanes requiring two or three occupants, are utilized in metropolitan areas throughout America. Driving bans and restrictions are nothing new.

Typical emergency vehicle restrictions must be imposed to make up for decades of conscious high-speed and reckless driving into the disaster zone of vulnerable oil dependence. Wasteful use of gasoline by needlessly heavy "show vehicles" driven by individuals guzzling more than their fair share of fuel as a status symbol will be the very first targets. Therefore, Hummers, Navigators, Explorers, and heavy non-commercially utilized pickup trucks will be immediately grounded until retrofitted for alt fuels and propulsion such as compressed natural gas (CNG), electric batteries, biofuel that does not injure agricultural yield, hydrogen gas, liquid ammonia fuel or any ethanol other than corn-derived. This initial restriction will unapologetically hit the most ostentatious gas guzzlers the hardest and first. Commercial weight vehicles, too often used as personal show cars, will only be driven by individuals who have secured a genuine commercial drivers license or who can prove that they qualify for one occupationally.

Hitting the big spenders and the sources of conspicuous gasoline overconsumption will actually lead the way to a retrofitting revolution that will benefit the entire nation. The owner of these expensive vehicles, typically the most affluent, will rush to ensure that they can get back up and running in their show cars. As they create the demand for retrofitting to flex fuel and alt fuel, the availability and cost will come down for all. In other words, status warfare will not be waged against ostentation. Hummers can keep humming, Navigators can keep navigating, and Escalades can keep escalading—so long as they do so using a fuel other than gasoline.

When one gas-guzzling car literally consumes twice the amount of another car, it hurts everyone because there is less fuel to go around. The same approach would be taken for those washing their cars or watering their lawns during a severe water shortage.

Retrofitting should favor all alternatives. No alt fuel or propulsion method need achieve supremacy. In locales where CNG, methanol, ethanol or biodiesel seems more apt, those should prosper. If electric vehicles are possible, they should be utilized. If recycled vegetable oils or non-agrifuel ethanol is most appropriate to the individual or area, it should be employed. Recent automotive history has shown that a range of fuels can be employed to operate a car—from hydrogen gas to ammonia to cellulosic ethanol.[21] The more diverse the alternatives, the better for all.

In the initial restrictions, the most fuel-efficient vehicles will be openly rewarded. The most fuel inefficient will be the highest priority for restriction and conversion, while the most fuel efficient will be the lowest priority. However, even the most fuel-efficient vehicles will need to retrofit away from gasoline within twelve months of the fuel emergency. Eventually, all vehicles will need to convert— the worst first.

Regulation 6: Overnight Fuel Stimulation. Maximum surge production by all domestic oil producers and at all domestic oil fields shall be mandated. All reasonable efforts shall be undertaken to encourage surge production among NAFTA treaty members Mexico and Canada, and among non-OPEC exporting nations. Federal subsidies to corn ethanol as well as importation levies upon Brazilian sugar ethanol shall be suspended. Caribbean Basin and Central American sugar ethanol shall be promoted.

DISCUSSION

Surge production is one of the pillars of the IEA's crisis plan. Appeals to OPEC members such as Saudi Arabia or the Gulf States will not succeed unless those nations fear threats to their own territorial security from hostile neighbors or terrorists. President George Bush's two stultifying visits to Saudi Arabia appealing for more oil production—missions openly called "hat-in-hand" by many in the media and oil industry observers alike—yielded naught.[22] Nor do IEA partners expect such appeals to be successful, which is why the IEA exists.

But America can mandate surge production from oilmen within its borders, request it from NAFTA partners and appeal for it from non-OPEC allies such as Norway. The main problem with surge production among allies is that a true blockage of the Apocalyptic Triangle will reduce world oil by as much as 25 percent. Seaborne oil will be cut by as much as 40 percent.[23] In such a circumstance, every nation from neighborly net exporters such as Canada to IEA allies such as Poland will be hard pressed to tend to their domestic needs. International cooperation will probably be token at best.

Overnight, gasoline extenders and replacements will be imperative. Ethanol will be vital, but not all ethanol is the same. Corn ethanol is politically expedient, especially during a presidential campaign when the Iowa Caucuses are all-important. But studies have shown that corn ethanol requires anywhere from 0.75 to 1.25 gallons of petroleum products or energy equivalents for every gallon of fuel produced. Yet corn ethanol fuel yields only two-thirds the mileage per gallon. Corn ethanol can only be used in a blend with genuine gasoline. In truth, corn ethanol can only be used as a gasoline extender if massive amounts of oil or energy equivalents are used in the process. For example, corn ethanol cannot be transported in pipelines, and instead requires conventional truck shipments. Moreover, the refining and production process requires even more petroleum in other industrial sectors, such as mining and railroad transport, to produce and convey the coal needed to feed the many dirty coal plants coming online to power the frenzied refining process.[24]

Most of all, the American government pays an unnecessary 51-cent-per-gallon subsidy for every gallon of ethanol, a price support achieved by a convergence of lobbying and commercial interests. This annual billion dollar–plus subvention is granted to the oil company blenders as an "incentive" to blend the ethanol yielded by such giant and questionable agribusiness concerns as Cargill, ConAgra and Archer Daniels Midland. The latter company, ADM, has been the subject of multiple criminal investigations, and in October 1996 it agreed to pay the largest criminal antitrust fine in history, $100 million, for price fixing of lysine. Cargill is privately owned and therefore not accountable as a publicly traded firm would be.[25] Corn ethanol is not in the hands of down home farmers, but the stuff of giant corporations.

However, Brazilian sugar cane ethanol is produced in a process ultimately eight times more efficient per gallon than corn ethanol. Corn ethanol requires blending with at least 15 percent traditional gasoline. But properly adjusted flex-fuel cars can operate on 100 percent Brazilian sugar ethanol. Brazil is geographically convenient for supplying the fuel hungry American Southeast. Yet the American importation of Brazilian ethanol is profoundly obstructed by a corn lobby–induced 54-cent-per-gallon special tax designed to keep this energy solution out of the country in favor of petroleum-dependent corn ethanol. Indeed, even American investment in Brazilian sugar cane ethanol has been thwarted by Washington-imposed restrictions. All those restrictions and per-gallon surcharges will need to be immediately suspended.[26]

Nor is Brazil the only source for sugar ethanol. Caribbean Basin islands can produce sugar-based ethanol and dispatch it to the automobile-congested Florida market, and elsewhere along the East Coast. Central American cane sugar ethanol shipments can also shuttle right through the Gulf of Mexico to the American Gulf Coast delivery systems.[27]

Alcohol fuels, of course, are derived from more sources than just sugar and corn. Methanol comes from wood. First discovered by the ancient Egyptians, methanol has for years been favored by race car drivers as a fuel for internal combustion that is safer than gasoline. Butanol, derived from a variety of sources from algae to biomass, could be rushed into production on a limited basis. The list of substitutes is long, and flex-fuel cars—after a small and relatively inexpensive engine modification—should be able to use admixtures, substitutes and extenders outside the realm of agrifuels so the fix will not impact the global food supply as corn ethanol currently does.[28]

Recycled vegetable oils are used by a growing following.[29] A homegrown industry purveying recovered fats and oils has been long awaiting the green light to expand. A crisis will ignite that industry.

Taken together, overnight stimulation of fuel extenders and replacements will dilute the addiction to foreign oil while we create the long-term shift away from petroleum.

Regulation 7: Inflate America. A program named Inflate America will broadly promote proper tire inflation to increase gasoline mileage. Inflate America will organize educational campaigns, assistance programs and enforcement efforts to ensure that motorists follow tire inflation guidelines.

DISCUSSION

Experts agree that better tire inflation could yield a 2 to 3 percent gain in miles per gallon.[30] If a protracted 10 percent shortfall could cause a major crisis, then the simple act of overseeing proper tire inflation is the surest, safest and fastest way of delivering measurable fuel savings. But tire inflation can be like dental flossing—everybody talks about it but not enough people do it.

To ensure that proper tire inflation takes effect where the rubber meets the road, Inflate America should be pursued with the same alacrity as efforts to stamp out drunk driving, compel seat belt use, reduce speeding and even stop highway littering. Efforts should include positive and proactive programs such as mandated tire inflation checking at gas stations, volunteer campaigns and mass advertising to promote the idea, designer tire gauges, and even patriotic tire inflation checking and adjustment services at major grocery stores and big box merchandise centers. The omnipresent high school car washes should include tire inflation checks.

Encouragement programs should be buttressed by enforcement. Sobriety checkpoints, seat belt vigilance and red light enforcement are well-known in America's cities. Regular vehicle inspection is mandated in many counties to verify engine and emission standards. Correct tire inflation should be added to the list.

Regulation 8: Carpool Enhancement. A program named Carpool America will widely promote shared rides both on an organized and ad hoc basis in daily commuting and other regular transportation. Staggered commute times to reduce travel and fuel-inefficient congestion shall be required, so long as they do not compromise the effected individuals, company or agency. All HOV2 lanes shall become HOV3 lanes.

DISCUSSION

Companies and localities have long accrued expertise in cultivating carpools. In addition, the nation has also witnessed a burgeoning "ride sharing" phenomenon propelled by the Internet, which can match riders with drivers at an impressive speed. What's more, in many cities, commuters have learned to simply queue up at *ad hoc* ride-sharing posts to pile into cars driven solo enabling them all to get to work in the fast lane, that is, the HOV lane. Those foundations can be greatly expanded by major employers ramping up their carpool programs.[31]

More than just carpools, companies or groups of neighboring companies can establish "employee muster points" in the suburbs and outlying areas. These muster points in local shopping centers and parking lots can be serviced by special drivers or designated employees who will drive directly to the company's front door, and then return. Employers can convert personal vans to flex-fuel or alt fuel and receive tax credit or grants for their participation.

Carpooling as a fuel saver will be magnified when employers and agencies adjust their start and finish times. Sometimes a 15- to 30-minute schedule adjustment can make all the difference between a rush hour crawl and fluid traffic. Bumper-to-bumper traffic means close to zero miles per gallon. Lessening the gasoline required to transit during a rush hour can transform worker habits and mindsets. The extra fuel consumed during a rush hour itself costs billions of dollars per year. A national study of Michigan traffic congestion published in 2007 discovered that the average Detroit trip takes approximately 38 percent longer during rush hour, and 14 percent longer even in the small city of Grand Rapids. That report calculated that Michigan's traffic congestion costs its drivers $2.3 billion annually in delays and wasted fuel.[32] Adjusting schedules will be more than compensated by decreased commute times and, therefore, greater overall productivity.

> **Regulation 9: Speed Limits.** A national speed limit of 55 MPH shall be imposed on all highways, except in rural counties with populations of fewer than 50,000.

DISCUSSION

America's love affair with vehicular speed emerges from an intersection of desire and distance. Detroit has always made powerful cars and sexed up their ability to achieve speed in crass appeals to accelerate. Indeed, power and speed have been the advertising focus of too many models, while fuel efficiency has been promoted by sedate messages. In prior decades, manufacturers actually installed standard speedometers in ordinary family cars featuring a 120 MPH demarcation. Prior to the first Arab Oil Embargo in 1973, 65-80 MPH speed limits could be routinely found throughout the country. Indeed, Montana, with vast wide open spaces, adopted a non-numeric rural speed limit allowing any velocity that was "reasonable and proper" under prevailing road conditions—in other words, no limit.[33]

After the first Arab Oil Embargo, the 55 MPH speed limit was imposed by federal law. Vastly unpopular, 55 MPH speed limit signs on country roads were commonly seen with light streaming through the bullet holes. Unpopular as the limits were, however, they were shown to dramatically reduce gasoline consumption as well as death and injury. Highway fuel savings by some estimates can soar as high as 15 percent when a 55 limit is observed. Nonetheless, by the late 1990s, the extreme public revulsion for 55 MPH limits, especially in such wide-open rural states such as Wyoming and Texas, led to the resurrection of 65-80 MPH speed limits. Montana even resumed its non-numeric speed limit, and that state's Supreme Court held that no numerical limit could be enforced. The state has since re-legislated a numerical 75 MPH limit on its fastest highways.[34]

Today, many professional drivers, including truck drivers, have learned that scrupulous adherence to what they previously denigrated as "the double-nickel"—the 55 MPH limit—delivers measurable savings.[35] By enforcing this limit, savings would dramatically help a national strategy to reduce consumption. Speed reductions are also a key tenet of the IEA's plan to reduce demand. In the process, lives will be saved, and some states have already reported reduced highway death tolls as expensive oil has impacted both the speed and volume of drivers.

By exempting the profound open sky rural routes in sparsely populated counties of such states as Wyoming, Montana and Texas, a balance is found for those who must traverse vast empty distances.

> **Regulation 10: Speed Enforcement Cameras.** Speed enforcement cameras will be installed on an accelerated basis on all federal interstates. Federal assistance shall be available to states, counties and cities for accelerated installation of speed enforcement cameras within their jurisdictions.

DISCUSSION

Universally reviled—and with good reason—speed enforcement cameras have proven to be a hated enforcement contraption. But they have also proven an effective tool in reducing speed, especially along fast thoroughfares, school zones and hospital zones. The cameras match a radar-detected speed violation to the offending license plate, and after a short delay, a fine inevitably arrives in the mail. Although a recent technological addition to the national traffic enforcement scene, the IEA has already listed such pesky cameras in its official armamentarium of fast demand restraint fundamentals.[36] Unfortunately, these noisome cameras work and must be used.

Regulation 11: Idling Restrictions. During an oil supply emergency, idling in excess of five minutes without a clear operational necessity shall be a violation.

DISCUSSION

An idling motor is sometimes necessary, especially when refrigerator trucks are operating to preserve their contents, when truck drivers are sleeping in their rigs, or when buses require either heat or air conditioning for their passengers. But a 2006 study by Argonne Laboratory calculated that some two billion gallons of fuel are burned each year by commercial vehicles, either during their normal workday or when utilized as overnight sleepers for the drivers. In 2000, overnight sleeping alone required 800 million gallons.

Cummins, a leading manufacturer of truck engines, concluded that the average truck driving 14 hours per day and traversing 100,000 miles per year burns some 1,500 extra gallons of diesel per vehicle due to idling. Many trucks wasted as much as 11 percent of their fuel during idling. Maintenance is also accelerated by idling. Measurable losses in fuel efficiency and financial efficacy are recorded after the engine has been idling for as little as five minutes.[37]

Yet studies show that by and large most daytime idling can be avoided altogether. Alternative energy supplies for heaters and air conditioners, such as hook-ups and auxiliary power units, can drastically reduce the necessity to use the engine for overnight cab comfort. Tamper-proof automatic engine shutdown devices are already being required by both air quality districts and petroleum-pinched trucking companies.[38] These measures should become mandatory.

Non-commercial idling would become an equal target for enforcement. Parents waiting at schools, spouses waiting at job sites and others would have to turn off their engines until their party arrives. Limousines and sedans that were able to operate vehicles within the new MPG restrictions would be among those deserving of the most intense enforcement. Idling limos, wasting gallon after gallon, have become a standard in big cities. Taxis and sedans in waiting pens such as most airports and hotel queues would be exempted because of their need to wait and incrementally advance.

More than just enforcement efforts akin to those employed against vehicle noise, tailpipe emission and intersection blocking, the campaign against idling can best be achieved by education campaigns. Not only does idling waste vast amounts of oil, but it also intensifies any single car's injury to the environment.

Importantly, hybrid-electric vehicles, which shut down when they idle, would of course be exempt.

Regulation 12: PTP Shuttles. Ad hoc Point-to-Point Shuttles shall be encouraged and implemented through fast, same-day licensing procedures requiring only a valid driver's license and a permissible, inspected alt-fuel vehicle—allowing willing individuals to shuttle passengers from point to point within a metropolitan area or from city to city, even across state lines. The government shall provide pool insurance to such shuttles, and "Good Samaritan" rules will apply in the event of an accident or other unforeseen liability. Such vehicles will be clearly identified as authorized PTP Shuttles.

DISCUSSION

Unlicensed, out-of-jurisdiction, or so-called "jitney" drivers are known in cities across America, running an important, if gray market, transportation service. Many airports, especially in the New York and Washington, D.C., areas, feature omnipresent unlicensed sedan drivers willing to pick up passengers outside normal channels. Point-to-Point Shuttles would bring these drivers and many others out of the shadows into the limelight, running short inexpensively-priced transits to and from subway and bus stops to local shopping centers, employer destinations and miscellaneous points of interest. At will, such spot licensed shuttle drivers could run small-dollar PTP circuits from city centers to the suburbs, between office complexes, from the stadium to the city neighborhood, up and down the freeway and anywhere else the need arose or as the traffic would bear.

PTP operations need not have schedules but could depart when the vehicle is full. Such transport would constitute vastly more than "a sedan service," and sedans would probably be in the minority. Usable vehicles would encompass any automobile or van permissible under the MPG regulations, whether they were family vans or simply four-passenger sedans. The unemployed, under-employed, students and those seeking extra temporary employment would help sprout an entire service sector freed from the onerous licensing procedures of city, county and federal bureaucracies. These operations could be as spontaneous as the snow shovelers that suddenly appear after a blizzard, or as organized as unlicensed jitney operations that cruise for passengers in many big cities.

In cities underserved by public transit, such as Southern California and South Florida, PTP shuttles would literally transform a region's mobility.

As valuable as in-city PTP will be intercity and interstate shuttles. State lines and municipal borders, each demarcating their own idiosyncratic jurisdictional licensing barriers, have been a major impediment to PTP transit. Under *The Plan*, regulatory prohibitions would dissolve between neighboring jurisdictions such as the New York/New Jersey/Connecticut tri-state region; between Suburban Maryland, Northern Virginia, and the District of Columbia; between the Chicago area, its suburban ring, and the adjacent Indiana industrial zone; and throughout the contiguous concrete metroplexes of Southern California, South Florida, Greater Las Vegas, Minnesota's Twin Cities and Dallas-Ft. Worth, to mention just a few. Hang the sign, wait for customers, charge a small fee and depart—it would be as simple as that.

In Israel, a famous discount shuttle service called the *Sherut*, or communal taxi, does just that. *Sherutim* depart every few moments between Jerusalem, Tel Aviv, Haifa and all points in-between. Four or five people pile into a sedan, and off they go. As such, *Sherutim* have long been a key underpinning of the Israeli public transportation system. Nothing is stopping the same type of service in America except jurisdictional and licensing barriers.

Regulation 13: No Charge or Deeply Discounted Public Transit Fares. Mass transit bus and rail fares, as well as regional commuter rail fares, shall be at no charge or deeply discounted, with government subsidies based on asset recoveries and other emergency revenue streams compensating for lost fare dollars.

DISCUSSION

A major tenet of the IEA emergency response protocol is shifting vehicular transportation to mass transit at a deep fare discount. Some of the most highly recommended IEA crisis plans even suggest 100 percent fare reductions. While steep fare reductions are assumed by the IEA, most members of the American Public Transit Association—representing the nation's public transit systems—are completely unaware of the expectation. The very notion surprised mass transit executives contacted on the question. Many had not heard of the IEA and did not know that the international treaty identifies highly discounted or completely no-charge mass transit as a key method of shifting off of oil in a crisis. These executives also wondered how they would recover the daily operating costs from the fare box, especially since reduced fares would profoundly expand usage.

Ironically, mass commuter migration from passenger vehicle to public transit has been in accelerated mode across the nation since 2007. By the summer of 2008, mass transit was already bursting with as much as a one-third increase over the preceding twelve-month period in some locales. Seats became hard to find. Commutes became "standing room only" for many, not just in the big cities but wherever mass transit rolled or railed.[39] Nonetheless, when asked in mid-2008, several major metropolitan systems were still in the throes of developing a contingency program to handle hordes of additional passengers in the event of an oil stoppage. As of summer 2008, they were still unprepared.

Deeply discounted or even free service would certainly strain any system. That would be the idea. Indeed, the public would flock to the turnstiles as soon as a serious crisis really took hold. To cope with surge usage, additional buses and longer trains could be pressed into service as routes were expanded and express routes developed to relieve the pressure. But if employers stagger commutes, as is often done, commuters can fill capacity outside the most concentrated peak times. Hence, longer trains and more buses can simply keep running instead of ebbing during the off-peak times. Indeed, "off-peak" and "peak" would glissando into each other.

For example, the Washington Metropolitan Area Transit Authority serves about 750,000 passengers daily by rail and bus, as of mid-2008. Its model subway and surface rail system operates six and eight car trains during the 90-minute morning and afternoon rush hours. WMATA representatives indicate that if commuters would stagger their rides outside the 90-minute window and if eight-car trains coursed all day and more frequently, the system could accommodate an additional 125,000 riders and perhaps more.[40]

That leaves unanswered how lost fare box revenues would be recovered. Answer: from windfall taxes and asset recoveries from automotive manufacturers and oil companies as well as the nation's monthly multibillion savings when oil consumption is radically reduced (these to be outlined in Chapter Six of this book). Add nearly two billion dollars in government subsidies to oil companies for blending corn ethanol that would be suspended, and the countervailing savings becomes apparent. Mass transit under *The Plan* would not just survive, it would thrive.

Regulation 14: Telecommuting. Appropriate telecommuting programs requiring at least one day per week among major employers and government agencies shall be mandatory where such a program will not compromise the effectiveness of either the designated individual or the affected company or agency.

DISCUSSION

Telecommuting has long been considered an economic and logistical advantage to corporate America when it does not compromise company or agency operations. Fuel savings is one of the central benefits. In many states, such as Connecticut, Florida and Virginia, telecommuting is already official government policy. Many states actually operate or promote telecommuting, either at local centers or at home, as an adjunct of their Department of Transportation. For example, in May 2008, California's governor signed an executive order encouraging Sacramento workers to telecommute at least one day per week during disruptive highway construction. Most universities and high-tech jobs consider telecommuting an inherent feature of employment. Telecommuting is everywhere in the hi-tech world, so much so that location is no longer an issue for many software and online employers.[41]

Telecommuting and remote employment are well-entrenched in the landscape of work. By expanding telecommuting to at least one day per week, significant and immediate reductions in petroleum use will be realized.

> **Regulation 15: RVs.** Within one week of an oil supply emergency declaration, no recreational vehicles shall be towed except by a vehicle operating on alternative fuel. All motorhomes and other motorized recreational vehicles shall be grounded until retrofitted for alternative fuel. Towed recreational vehicles shall not be permitted except by a retrofitted vehicle.

DISCUSSION

Recreational vehicles are the single most voracious highway source of miles per gallon gasoline overconsumption. Mileage for motorhomes, that is, self-drivable RVs, averages between 5 and 12

MPG. Motorhomes use more gasoline per mile than Hummers, Bentleys and Rolls Royces. RV mileage hits the very bottom rung when traversing slopes rather than straightways. Of the estimated eight million RVs in America, approximately two million of them are motorhomes, each traveling some 3,000 to 6,000 miles annually, depending upon the year, the price of gasoline and other conditions. Usage tightened profoundly in 2008.[42]

The other estimated six million RVs are so-called "towables," that is, campers and similar vehicular appendages, from minor "fifth-wheelers" to large customized live-ins. These loads, hitched behind family vehicles, reduce the fuel efficiency of the passenger cars, SUVs and pick-ups towing them by as much as a third, depending upon the weight of the towable and the terrain traveled, according to industry experts. Hence, a 20 MPG family vehicle can become a 10 MPG vehicle while towing a camper.[43] The extra gasoline consumed is not even calculated by the Department of Energy. But with six million such towed vehicles, the cumulative total must be considered an important factor.

Retired RV owners, people often faced with no vehicular options, and often few resources, have been willing to scrimp on food and curtail their destinations in order to preserve their cherished lifestyle. Indeed, the RV life is as central to the independent American spirit as the concept of freewheeling travel itself. But unable to afford the skyrocketing price of fuel, beleaguered RV owners are shaving tow weight to save miles per gallon, their own dinner menus to save money, and their favorite itineraries to save fuel—all to maintain their annual traditions. Some contacted RV owners expressed bitterness that their industry and its national association let them down so dramatically, ignoring a generation of warnings about the escalating oil squeeze, a generation during which motorized RVs and the private vehicles towing campers could have been retrofitted to flex fuel, with alternative fuels developed.[44]

Of the various industry sources contacted, the Recreational Vehicle Industry Association (RVIA) was among the most defensive about its members' unhappiness—and the most unrealistic about the realities of today's oil crisis. Pointing straight to Detroit for blame, an RVIA spokesman denied any responsibility for neglecting the growing RV pain at the pump. The spokesman declared that RV manufacturers merely purchase engines and chasses from Detroit and had no duty to alert their owners to switch to alt fuels. More than that, experts at the RVIA did not know anything about the IEA, what constituted an oil emergency under existing protocols or how much oil the USA consumed and where it came from. RV industry experts instead declared that at the height of any oil shortage emergency, gasoline consumption and use should just randomly be left to the individual and not prioritized by need.[45] Hence, in a rationing crisis, disproportionate RV consumption would be on the same footing as the need to get to work, rush to the hospital or respond to a fire.

Ironically, no community is better equipped to take advantage of retrofitting to flex-fuel and alt fuel than RV owners. Many are already equipped with CNG, propane and electrical hook-ups. They routinely carry heavy gear and extra tanks of propane. Spacious RV campgrounds, generally already outfitted for energy hookups, could easily become depots for alt fuel. And, RV owners are often adept at mechanical and automotive tinkering.

New lighter towables are being designed for a lesser mileage hit on passenger vehicles. The newest motor homes will achieve as much as 15 or 20 MPG.[46] But it will be years before these updated models achieve a significant market presence. Until that time, RV owners can help spearhead a transportation revolution by virtue of the fact that their temporarily banished vehicles have the greatest chance of quickly coming back to the highway and scooting to the front of the alt-fuel parade.

Regulation 16: Marine Restrictions on yachts, speed boats and non-commercial pleasure craft. Within one week of an oil supply emergency declaration, all non-commercial marine craft, including but not limited to private yachts, speed boats, recreational vessels and personal watercraft, shall be unable to refuel in the Continental United

States, except in an emergency, until retrofitted to accept alternative fuel or propulsion systems.

DISCUSSION

As defensive as the RV vehicle industry was, representatives of the American Boating Association (ABA) understood that in any genuine fuel rationing crisis, all recreational consumption, such as that utilized by private boating and yachting, would be the first to be sidelined until retrofitting. The ABA represents some 15 million watercraft enthusiasts. Membership includes a range of watercraft operators, from those who sail with the wind, using a mere pittance of oil in their generators, to pleasure craft owners who enjoy day trips, to the ostentatious mega-yachts that voraciously drain the national supply by drinking hundreds of gallons per hour just to transport a handful of partygoers.[47]

Unlike the RVIA, an ABA spokesman knew about the IEA, understood completely how vulnerable the nation's oil supply was, and declared that many in his community would be the among first to step up to the pier and convert to flex-fuel, alt fuel and alternative forms of propulsion. Indeed, the spokesman assured, many boaters hit by exorbitant gas bills are already exploring alternatives including wind, solar and alcohol fuels. Boaters, like the RV community, could help lead the alt fuel revolution. Boat and yacht owners are known for their abundant disposable income, ready ingenuity and frequent visits to islands capable of producing sugar fuels. As such, a marine community anxious to return to the water could populate the coastlines with an alt fuel infrastructure. That infrastructure would fuel not only their vessels but the automobiles used to shuttle to and from the dock.

Most emergency IEA member legislation calls for limiting recreational marine access to petroleum during an oil crisis. But that restriction could be the shortest, most beneficial ban required by *The Plan.*

Regulation 17: Home Heating. Within one week of an oil

supply emergency declaration, the Northeast Home Heating Strategic Petroleum Reserve shall be drained to exhaustion and not refilled. All use of oil for home heating will be discontinued as soon as practicable after such a declaration. An immediate census of home heating oil consumers will be undertaken to identify and schedule conversion to other forms of home energy, including geothermal, natural gas, propane, solar, wind, grid-based electric or other sources, with all such conversions receiving 100 percent financial assistance from the federal government. Oil powered appliances shall be replaced with fuel-efficient appliances that do not require petroleum, such as "tankless" natural gas water heaters.

DISCUSSION

Approximately 7.7 million households in American heat their homes with oil. Almost 70 percent of them—about 5.3 million households—are found in the Northeast. As such, they are most vulnerable to a disruption, especially during winter. The only protection for oil heated homes in the event of a disruption is the two million barrels found in the Northeast Home Heating Strategic Petroleum Reserve—enough to sustain a few days of winter usage. Yet these households require some 7 billion gallons per year, or about 1.8 barrels of oil annually. Heating oil is distillate and converts to a different gallon-per-barrel ratio than gasoline.[48]

Using oil to heat homes is ancient. Under *The Plan*, census-style advisors would visit home oil customers door-to-door, assess their needs and recommend fast fixes. If necessary, individualized counseling and even hands-on assistance would be rendered. Alternate sources of energy from geothermal to standard natural gas or solar would be recommended, depending upon the wishes of the consumer and advisability for the oil-dependent residence. Modern, highly efficient replacement appliances would be part of the retrofit. Financial incentives, such as tax credits, grants and loans, would be provided to make the transition as painless as possible.

The Northeast Home Heating Strategic Petroleum Reserve would be drained and go out of business.

Regulation 18: Oil-Related and Automotive Lobby Contacts. Governmental contacts with agents or industry associations representing oil producing or consumption interests, and/or with representatives of the automotive industry, will be subject to strictures identical to those contained within the Foreign Agents Registration Act. In addition, such contacts shall require ten-day advance notice to the public and be held in a public forum open to the press and public. Such contacts should be televised on appropriate cable TV systems and made available for network TV coverage.

DISCUSSION

Of all the regulations proposed, none is more controversial or indispensable than restricting, controlling and shining daylight and public scrutiny on contacts between government and oil-related lobbyists or agents. Unless representatives of oil producers or consuming associations and the automotive industry are kept out of the rescue process, all the well-chiseled proposals in the world will come to naught.

Indeed, the country has found itself in the present petroliferous predicament because lobbyists from oil and automotive industries have waged war upon the public for the narrow benefits of their sponsors. For these lobbyists, the enemy has been good ideas, good solutions and good alternatives to our addiction to oil. The victor has been the status quo, the perpetrators of the problem, those unwilling to change, the inflictors of bad technology, unworkable ideas and stagnation. The vanquished are quite simply the public at large, and indeed the world.

Lobbyists only receive 49 percent of the blame. Congress and regulators own the rest of that dubious distinction. Lobbyists are understandably paid to represent special interests. But the legislators and regulators who have dishonored their duty of saving the country will never be able to justify what they have done. History will record their harmful votes and non-votes.

To counteract the well-entrenched history of collusive lobbyists, legislators and regulators, the Foreign Agents Registration Act (FARA) is only the beginning, but a good one nonetheless. FARA dates from 1938 when America acted to register the propagandizing efforts of Nazi Germany. The legislation has been updated and expanded regularly to encompass more and more categories of foreign agents.[49]

FARA was specifically designed to keep representatives of foreign interests at bay, restrict their contact and make such contacts—even casual ones, such as leafleting, advertising and phone calls—part of a public record to be scrutinized. Under FARA, covered individuals and agencies must register with the Department of Justice and report all contacts with governmental sources and even the media. The rule covers all representatives of foreign interests, from publicists and lawyers to managers and often ordinary service people.[50]

FARA extends to such diverse entities as a foreign government, a national airline, a foreign corporation or philanthropic association, even overseas artistic associations. As such, FARA registration is required for the ladies who work for Hadassah Hospital in Israel, the manager of the gourmet kitchen in the French Embassy, publicists for the coffee growers of Ethiopia and the British-American Chamber of Commerce as well as the more obvious agents, lawyers and spokesmen of embassies and consulates.[51]

Additional precedents for a "Sunshine Law" approach came to the national fore during the 2008 presidential campaign when one candidate, Democrat Barack Obama, actually suggested that negotiations with the health industry be conducted only in televised forums. The idea was to forbid the type of private discussions that have so typified the decades-long legacy of pro-industry health legislation. The June 2008 deliberations by the Democratic National Committee to arbitrate between contenders Senators Hillary Clinton and Barack Obama were broadcast gavel-to-gavel on C-SPAN and cable TV.[52] For decades, such political maneuvering has been conducted in smoke-filled back rooms. Opening the process to real-time public scrutiny was a revolutionary step in American politics and democracy. The same disinfecting sunshine needs to be applied to the all-powerful interests who have kept our nation and the world addicted to oil.

Indeed, the history of clandestine and stealthy activities of the automotive industry to undermine public transit, sequester innovation, destroy incentives to improve gas mileage and subvert alternatives to petroleum is one that literally chronicles America's petroaddiction.

Henry Ford's cheap Model-T and the proliferation of well-entrenched electric cars were thwarted in the first dozen years of the 20th century by secretive automobile monopolies. Then, in 1914, when Henry Ford and Thomas Edison teamed up to establish inexpensive, electric automobiles to be serviced by a national network of simple recharging stations and home generation, internal combustion interests subverted their every move. Ultimately, false engineering reports gave way to arson, and Edison's complex was burned to the ground.[53]

In the 1930s and 1940s, GM led a criminal conspiracy along with Mack Truck, Firestone, Standard Oil and Philips Petroleum to secretly fund a front company called National City Lines. Run by five uneducated Minnesota bus drivers functioning as front men, National City Lines purchased electric trolley systems across the country. Once National City Lines took ownership, it tore up the tracks, burned the trolley cars and replaced them with oil-drinking, smoke-belching buses. Eventually, in 1949, GM, its cohorts and a number of company executives were prosecuted, convicted and fined for criminal conspiracy for their broad, years-long scheme to dismantle mass transit and replace it with an oil-dependent network in some 40 cities.[54]

Even as GM was undermining clean, electric mass transit in America in the 30s and 40s, the company was secretly helping the Hitler regime prepare to conquer Europe and wage war against the U.S. Using secret interlocking boards of directors and executive committees, all personally directed by GM's president, Alfred

Sloan, GM motorized the Third Reich and its military. Until that time, Germany suffered from a horse-drawn military, and even that capability was dismantled by the Versailles Treaty after World War I. Shortly after Hitler took over Germany in 1933, GM asked *der Führer* for permission to help the Reich prepare for the next war and help restore the Germany's bankrupt economy and Depression-wracked workforce. Hitler, a car enthusiast who knew that Germany needed to become motorized, agreed. GM energetically produced the Blitz truck for the 1939 *Blitzkrieg*. The company played a key role in Germany's launch of the war by pre-positioning vehicle replacement parts along the Polish border in the days leading up to the September 1, 1939, invasion. GM also helped produce German tanks, torpedoes and JU-88 bombers, partnering with the Nazis in a war against all of humanity waged from land, sea and air.[55]

Then in 1974, when Congress tried to expose the sordid details of both National City Lines and the alliance with Hitler, GM intimidated Congress itself to suppress the report.[56]

In recent years, automotive interests helped secure a special $25,000 tax write-off for vehicles weighing more than 6,000 pounds, this ostensibly to encourage commercial work vehicles. Detroit exploited the provision to mass produce such gargantuan gas guzzlers as Ford's Navigator, GM's Escalade and the GM Hummer. Even under revised regulations, the notorious Hummer H1, achieving an average of only 11 MPG and sporting a sticker price of more than $106,000, could reap a tax write-off of nearly $61,000 within the first twelve months after regular depreciation, bonus depreciation and then the $25,000 heavy vehicle write-off. In some cases, the entire purchase price of a heavy SUV could be written off.[57]

One Ft. Lauderdale businessman declared, "How could I not buy one—it was free."[58]

Ironically, the Hummer H1 was discontinued by GM for lack of customers.[59]

The massive loophole, dubbed "The Hummer Tax Loophole," was mocked by at least one network as "a tax credit on steroids."

Congressional watchdog groups estimated the Hummer loophole cost taxpayers between $840 million and $987 million for every 100,000 of the 50 or so qualifying vehicle models sold.[60] Billions in tax money annually that could have proliferated clean alternatives has been spent each year to dramatically worsen our addiction to oil—this with the active participation of the nation's wealthiest doctors, lawyers, accountants and entertainers. The enzyme for this addiction was a well-honed lobbying campaign on Capitol Hill.

In another extraordinary Congressional act against American energy independence in favor of Detroit special interests, the tax credit for the most fuel-efficient hybrids manufactured by Toyota and Honda was capped at 60,000 vehicles. Because fuel-conscious Americans began flocking to such high mileage vehicles as the Toyota Prius over gas guzzlers manufactured by GM and Ford, Congress imposed an arbitrary legal limit of 60,000 vehicles qualified for the tax credit. That 60,000 limit was reached by California and Ohio-based Toyota and Honda long ago. As of January 2009, Toyota and Honda hybrids will not be allowed a tax credit.[61]

With the highly favored hybrids of Honda and Toyota out of the way, Detroit automakers were free to create heavy SUV "hybrids" that still achieve mileage only in the teens but are now qualified for a tax credit. By using the term "hybrid," Detroit can depict these gas guzzling vehicles as "green" or even good for oil independence. The Orwellian advertising is permitted even though such fuel-inefficient vehicles achieve less mileage than a typical non-hybrid but fuel-efficient Honda Accord or Civic. This hurtful tax loophole was stealthily accomplished by GM lobbyists, literally when many were not looking.[62]

The list of legislation ensuring our oil addiction scrolls down into the most collusive and unilluminated shadows of congressional misbehavior. Consider corn ethanol subsidies of 51 cents per gallon to oil companies for a fuel requiring a gasoline base and possibly more than a gallon of petroleum products to produce and distribute. Consider prohibitive 54-cent-per-gallon levies and other taxes imposed upon Brazilian, Central American and Caribbean sugar ethanol, which vehicles can use in a 100 percent oil-free blend. Consider hydrogen fuel cell research and development stagnated and undermined by token billions spread out over half of a decade to sound as though action is being taken when in fact it is being delayed.[63]

In the meantime, oil companies are granted billions per year in special tax breaks and subsidies to encourage drilling.[64] New drilling is like a taxpayer plan to help locate new sources of cigarettes—or, as some have observed, heroin.

Iowa corn producers, Detroit carmakers, oil companies and the other forces of petroaddiction must be kept out of the fix. They will destroy it, dilute it, distract it, dismantle it, or divert it. Only a national Katrina moment, only a collective "Dubai ports" outrage can move the public to demand genuine action without political circumlocution, parsed excuses or subversions concocted on the golf course or in the dead of night by lobbyists and other oil agents. No one knows if that collective, no-excuses moment will come when gasoline reaches $10 per gallon or $15—or whether it will require a protracted stoppage to ignite the public.

But if lobbyists are not excluded from the rescue plan, then any plan will be doomed. In that case, this book and all its careful recommendations and precedents can be thrown away. However, then it remains unknown if city trucks will be able to obtain the fuel to pick up the trash—or if anyone will have the gas to pick up the pieces.

CHAPTER FIVE

Week Three— The Retrofitting Revolution

America's current ability to save itself by retrofitting oil-dependent vehicles is bleak. Worse than bleak. Short-term driving restrictions, exhaustion of the Strategic Petroleum Reserve and the many other special, seemingly onerous regulations of *The Plan* will be a fruitless re-arrangement of deck chairs on the Titanic without the indispensable simultaneous program: retrofitting, now also called "upfitting."

Kicking the oil addiction means more than just buying spiffy new cars powered by batteries, hydrogen, CNG or numerous other alternatives. If the nation suddenly manufactures, and consumers then purchase, a million new electric, hydrogen, and CNG cars each month, at the end of a year more than 250 million gas guzzling vehicles will remain on the nation's roads to continue drinking oil.

America and the world will require a crash retrofitting revolution to survive any traumatic shift off oil. But the country is completely unprepared to even start.

Retrofitting—or upfitting—a vehicle can be a simple or complex operation, relatively cheap or expensive, quick or slow. It all depends upon the vehicle, the retrofitter, the vehicle's intended use and the type of retrofit a vehicle will undergo. A pivotal question is upfit to what? What is the best choice: CNG, ethanol, methanol, electric or any of a dozen other varieties of alternative?

The mistake would be to dictate a fuel conversion or propulsion preference. The world's alternative fuel possibilities for conversion are numerous. Many of them are well-entrenched, decades-old technologies, some more than a century old. We do not need to reinvent the wheel as much as exhume it from where it was buried during the 10 decades of the 20th century by corporate and political avarice. Just as guilty are a glissando of public policy failures that continue to reverberate like slow-motion shots heard around the world—traveling not at the speed of sound but the velocity of fog. Now we are enveloped in energy confusion with almost zero visibility. The key partner in this carefully stage-managed addiction has been the public itself. Society ratified Detroit's prestidigital misdirection. Gleefully, without a gun to its head, society followed Detroit's piper toward the flashing lights and thumping music, adoring glitzy SUVs and the sexed-up yet reckless manufacture of the worst possible vehicles for a planet ever-conscious it was fast running out of oil. No one ever questioned the man behind the curtain. His elixir, the fume of internal combustion, was oh so intoxicating. The seats were plush. The stereo was surround sound. The sense of machismo became a cross-gender phenomenon.

But now the truth is known. We were purchasing our own predicament on the installment plan. The world is trapped in an oil line—no butting or departures allowed.

So to be free, when King Oil dies, we cannot hail: "The King is Dead, Long Live the King." There shall be no new fuel king. The monarchy of petroleum will be replaced not with another dictator but with a fuel democracy. Fortunately, there are many contenders.

HYDROGEN could become the ultimate alternative fuel, especially when used in a hydrogen fuel cell. However, hydrogen fuel cells are such complex and expensive devices that replacing a standard internal combustion engine with a hydrogen fuel cell is basically as impracticable as converting a school bus into a motorcycle. More technically feasible is converting a vehicle's existing engine to accept hydrogen gas carried in a heavy cylinder. Urban buses, tractors, state police cars and other commercial and experimental vehicles have been converted to hydrogen gas as demonstration projects. But because the storage tanks are large, generally heavy, expensive and in short supply, hydrogen gas is an unrealistic near term conversion option for personal vehicles. So hydrogen is a poor choice for mass upfit.[1]

AMMONIA, a compound rich in hydrogen, is one of the most universally manufactured and available substances on earth. In China, one finds more anhydrous ammonia dispensing outlets than gasoline stations. Iowa alone offers some 800 retail ammonia dispensing stations. At room temperature, liquid anhydrous ammonia contains 50 percent more hydrogen per gallon than even cryogenic liquid hydrogen itself. Indeed, Ammonia has been officially trademarked as "the other hydrogen." Ammonia can be produced from simply water and air using any renewable or nuclear energy source that generates electricity. As a fuel, it produces no tailpipe $CO2$ emissions. Cheap to process and distribute, Ammonia, can efficiently deliver its hydrogen to both international combustion engines and automotive fuel cells. Anhydrous ammonia-fueled motors and automobiles have existed since the 1800s. Powerful and efficient, ammonia propelled the famous X-15 rocket airplane in the 1960s.[2]

In 1970, German propulsion scientist Karl Kordesch, smuggled into New Jersey from post-Nazi Germany by Operation Paperclip, proved an average car could be retrofitted to run on ammonia. Kordesch lashed six ammonia cylinders to the roof of his four-passenger Austin A-40 and installed a fuel cell in the trunk, thus creating the world's first hydrogen automobile that actually operated day-in day-out. Kordesch drove that Austin A-40 as his personal car with a regular state license plate on public roads for thousands of miles during a three-year period. His car enjoyed a 180-mile range. As of the summer of 2008, the vehicle was parked in Kordesch's garage in Ohio, still in operating condition and ready to roll again if revived with fresh fuel cells. Kordesch's breakthrough was ignored by the big automakers.[3]

But the spirit of Kordesch's retrofitting genius continues among an entire community of engineers steeped in ammonia propulsion. Among the many advocates is Ted Hollinger, formerly of Ford Motor Co, who heads up the Hydrogen Engine Center in Iowa. Right now he creates and converts ammonia-powered off-road vehicles and specialty engines, such as fork lifts, stationary generators, and machine motors. Hollinger says he has steered clear of standard vehicle upfitting to avoid competing against the Detroit carmakers. But, Hollinger said, with the proper financing he could ramp up to mass retrofit ordinary household cars or fleet vehicles to ammonia internal combustion.[4]

Ammonia upfits require a new ignition system to spark at a higher temperature, new lightweight storage tanks and some other engine modifications. This type of upfit is especially suited to heavier vehicles that can carry tanks in their cargo areas, or on the roof. Hollinger speculates the cost could be $10,000 per vehicle, perhaps much cheaper if volume fleet orders kick in. Each vehicle upfit might take a few weeks. If he had enough capital and notice to hire, train and ramp up, Hollinger thinks he might be transform 10,000 internal combustion vehicles per year to cheap, abundant ammonia.[5]

Like all combustible fuels, ammonia is an extremely hazardous substance with a record of spills, fires, and injury, mainly from equipment failure. Storage and usage can be a major issue as it is with all fuels. Ammonia fuel proponents are working now to proliferate the same level of industrial and consumer safety training that has been developed for petroleum, natural gas, propane and hydrogen.

ALCOHOL fuels, many of which are known as ethanol, are probably among the best alternatives because of their renewable nature. Each of the alcohol fuels comes with its own high-pressure lobby group or advocacy community. Ethanols are the leading contenders.

Most people know that corn ethanol has taken center stage in the national debate as an alternative to petroleum. What began as a 10 and 15 percent "gasoline extender" has become elevated to a potential major ingredient in a gallon of "gas." E85, for example, is an emerging blend of automobile fuel composed of 85 percent ethanol and only 15 percent gasoline. Dedicated E85 pumps have been established at gas stations countrywide, mainly in the Midwest's corn-rich farm belt.[6]

At first blush, ethanol derived from corn appears to be a solution from America's heartland, a win-win proposition in the struggle to free the world from harmful hydrocarbons and politically embroiling fuel. But American corn ethanol cannot stand on its own. Corn ethanol actually depends upon the continued use of petroleum and by necessity increases petroleum consumption and greenhouse gases. Many experts in the contentious ethanol debate argue that corn ethanol simply uses more petroleum or energy equivalents than it saves.

For example, a key series of studies was conducted by Tad Patzek, a University of California geoengineer, and David Pimentel, a Cornell University expert in life sciences, energy, and sustainable agriculture. Pimentel's and Patzek's numerous, peer-reviewed studies assert that, "ethanol production using corn grain required 29 percent more fossil energy than the ethanol fuel produced." Those energy expenditures cover a range of hydrocarbon users from the diesel-burning tractors and combines on the farm to the ordinary trucks needed for transport to and from the industrial centers.[7]

"In plain words," Pimentel explained, "1.29 gallons of petroleum or petroleum equivalents are needed to produce one gallon of corn ethanol." Even a study by Argonne Labs touted by the corn ethanol industry declares that .75 gallons of petroleum or petroleum equivalents are needed to produce one gallon of corn ethanol.[8]

But other forms of ethanol and alcohol fuels are attractive. For example, Brazilian cane sugar is a major source of ethanol and can be used in a 100 percent form. Unfortunately for the American driver, the importation of Brazilian ethanol is severely restricted by a collection of corn-lobbied Congressional measures including a 54-cent per gallon punitive tariff. At the same time, corn ethanol receives a multi-billion dollar federal subsidy paid directly to the oil companies. Until summer 2008, it was 54 cents per gallon, which was then reduced to 45 cents per gallon as corn ethanol production volume surged. But it still diverts billions in federal money.[9]

Methanol is derived from wood among other substances. Butanol comes from beets and other feedstocks including a variety of biomass, or living matter. Cellulosic ethanol is distilled from fibrous waste including woody refuse, paper trash, switchgrass and other seemingly useless products.[10] Numerous other alcohol fuel variants exist and are useful as long as they are not agrifuel, such as corn ethanol, which has contributed to soaring food prices and fears of starvation.

To utilize a range of alcohol fuels, that is, to become flex-fuel, vehicles need a series of modifications, according to John Lauckner, a GM vice president in charge of alternative fuels. First, a sensing system must be installed to determine the exact type of fuel or blend being burned, from traditional gasoline to ethanol or any combination. Then everything the alcohol fuel comes into contact with—from fuel lines to the tank, must be replaced with new materials compatible with alcohol. For example, rubber seals are attacked by alcohol, according to Lauckner. High pressure injectors can be gummed up, he says. For any upfit, the entire fuel system would need to be replaced. New engine controls to determine the volatility, viscosity and blend of the fuel would also be needed.[11]

Some say a flex-fuel upfit would be as inexpensive to install as $1,000 per car. It depends, of course, on the vehicle, the volume pricing of the upfitter and the type of fuel anticipated. A program of mass upfitting would bring costs down for any upfitting center.[12]

SECOND GENERATION BIOFUEL covers a broad group of alternative fuels derived from various plant matter, overlapping some of the alcohols, such as cellulosic and biomethane, but increasingly deserving a class of its own. While *agrifuels* such as corn ethanol, undermine the global food supply, some of the more fascinating so-called "second generation biofuels" arise from palm oil, algae, recovered trash, recycled edible fats and oils, various forms of vegetable fuel, pond scum and laboratory-raised bacteria. These exotic new fuels, rapidly being developed, are advanced enough to use today to extend traditional petroleum by as much as 20 percent, and already, some second generation biofuels are potent enough to power motors without being blended with any gasoline at all.[13]

NATURAL GAS, also known as compressed natural gas or CNG, represents one of the most viable of the immediate upfits. CNG is the gas in common kitchen ovens. In most parts of America, CNG is routinely piped into homes. Substantially cleaner than oil and supplied by mainly North American sources in this country, CNG is a bridge technology capable of delivering petroleum freedom to thousands of households. Home CNG fueling devices can quickly sever dependence on gas stations. More than 8.4 million CNG automobiles manufactured by major automakers or upfitted are operated throughout the world as of summer 2008. Many American city buses coast-to-coast have long operated on pure CNG. Unfortunately, except for a token 90 CNG automobiles per month made by Honda, the major car companies refuse to sell Americans the same CNG vehicles they manufacture for many other countries.[14]

Switching to CNG internal combustion takes a few days and requires new fuel systems and installation of a new tank. It is especially suited to heavier vehicles and fleets. The technology and practice of CNG upfitting is well-established. The CNG upfit industry-in-waiting is looking for a steady green light from government and market forces.[15]

ELECTRIC conversions probably represent the ultimate upfit. While many in the automotive establishment dismiss the idea as fundamentally impossible from a practical standpoint, an entire community of determined electric vehicle upfitters is emerging. Electric car makers—from Detroit's GM to Israel's Better Place—are scrambling to mass produce the endless supply of new high-tech batteries that will power thousands of electric vehicles (EVs) beginning in 2010 when many new model rollouts are expected.[16]

But not a few home-grown electric upfitters are unwilling to wait, because electric conversions are viable today. Some of these impatient upfitters are using standard, abundantly available, old-fashioned, low-tech lead batteries. One start-up, known as Evaira, formed by Phillips Aerospace, a small California engineering firm, is rushing into the field with a basic, old-fashioned lead acid battery pack, powering a low-cost self-commutating, "brushed DC motor." The old gasoline motor will be thrown away. A newly installed electric drive will be governed by an Electric Vehicle Management seated in place of the radiator, this to create a central nervous system for the vehicle. The new fully electric vehicle, with a 30-mile range, will recharge in five hours from a standard wall socket either overnight in the garage or during the work day while parked.[17]

Evaira vice president Randy Dunn says the firm can convert a vehicle in two weeks, charging about $17,000. The company will then recertify the car as pure electric. The limited use batteries are expected to last one or two years. Evaira will replace them for $3,000 each. The company has partnered with a lead battery source to provide an endless amount of recyclable lead batteries. Although Dunn and his colleagues are aerospace engineers—or perhaps because they are—Evaira asserts that the process is not rocket science. "This is simple stuff," Dunn says flatly.[18]

Lead batteries are just a temporary expedient to jump start conversions before the end of 2008. By 2009, Evaira expects to use a sophisticated lithium manganese battery, safer than the common lithium ion versions that contain cobalt and have been known to unexpectedly explode in laptops.[19]

Evaira's prices for vehicle conversion will dramatically reduce with volume and improvement of the motors, electronics and batteries. In the meantime, the converted vehicles will be zero emission and zero gasoline. Evaira is just one of many that call themselves "mom and pop" upfitters waiting for volume to bring them into the limelight and onto the main street. What could stop the rapid expansion in upfitting? What makes the outlook so completely bleak? Answer: the country is simply not ready—and not even ready to get ready.

The most dramatic single factor in America's lack of readiness is the virtual non-existence of an upfitting or retrofitting industry. In fact, "industry" is the wrong word. There is merely a disparate community of small businesses and mom and pop upfitting operations working out of garages, back yards and shops. No national association of upfitters exists. Upfitters are merely "appearing" out of economic desire, patriotic duty, green devotion or all of the above.

The best entrenched conversion program in America is for natural gas. Yet about six small CNG conversion companies do most of the upfits. They are all swamped with requests they cannot fulfill.

Among the largest of the small CNG upfitters is Dallas-based BAF Technologies. The company's vice president Bill Calvert says his small firm will struggle to upfit some 880 vehicles in 2008, up from about 500 the year before. Looking forward, the firm is scrambling to find the capital and wherewithal to expand enough to retrofit as many as 2,000 vehicles in 2009. The company is so flooded with requests beyond its resources, that as recently as summer 2008, it hadn't updated its website for the prior two years. Moreover, BAF Technologies won't convert just any vehicle that comes its way. As of summer 2008, BAF only does natural gas conversions on a select group of vehicles. It concentrates on Ford pickups and trucks, namely F-150s, F-250s, and F-350s, as well as the E-350 van and the E-450 truck, plus a limited number of Ford passenger cars, such as the Lincoln Town Car, Crown Victoria and the Mercury Marquis. It also converts a select few GM vehicles, such as the C5500 truck. The cost is approximately $14,000 per vehicle which is subject to counterbalancing tax credits. BAF does not upfit to flex-fuel, electric or any system other than CNG.[20]

BAF's Calvert would like to ramp up to convert thousands of trucks and automobiles. But ramping up cannot be done overnight. It would take weeks and months of non-stop expansion: facilities, components, trainees and money.[21]

TransEco Energy Corp. is another leading CNG upfitter so overwhelmed by the demand that the company turns away more than 100 requests each week. The company can convert a Ford Focus for about $8,000, and can accommodate Ford pick-up trucks and large Chevrolet vans such as the Savanna. About half of the conversion cost is defrayed by tax credits and other incentives. Ad hoc company spokesman Par Neiburger is also wondering when his firm can dramatically expand its operation. "If the floodgates were open," says Neiburger, "we would try to convert those 100 per week."[22]

What is keeping the floodgates clamped shut? A key obstacle to mass CNG conversion is the Environmental Protection Agency (EPA) and the California Air Resources Board (CARB). Unknown to most who want to get off of oil, EPA and CARB emission standards make the effort a Herculean, almost intimidating task. Complying with the Clean Air Act requires that any upfitter obtain certification one "engine family" at a time. An "engine family" refers to the type of engine that vehicle manufacturers use in a variety of makes and models. That certification can cost between $50,000 and $100,000 per engine family and take months. Only a few engine types have been approved. Moreover, the certifications must be renewed almost annually. "If we don't get certification first," says Neiburger, "we can be fined substantially every day for 'tampering with a federal emissions device.'"[23]

Consequently, throughout the summer of 2008, Trans-Eco dramatically reduced its upfitting volume to concentrate its personnel on additional emissions testing for more conversion kits. During the summer, the company sent out dramatic rejection letters to hundreds seeking to get off oil and onto CNG.[24] The letter reads:

DUE TO THE DRAMATIC INCREASES IN GASOLINE AND DIESEL PRICES WE ARE FIELDING AN EXTREMELY LARGE VOLUME OF CALLS

I apologize, but due to current EPA regulations, we can currently only do conversions on certain vehicles. We can and will do conversions on individual cars that have available EPA certified conversion kits. Please be advised that in accordance with EPA (Environmental Protection Agency) Memorandum 1A, it is not legal to do a conversion on a vehicle that does not have an EPA certified conversion kit. Consequently, we can only legally convert certain vehicles. The conversion of a vehicle to a Natural Gas Vehicle involves the acquisition and subsequent installation of the conversion kit, and then the upfitting of CNG tanks. Technologically speaking, we can convert any vehicle and can acquire a conversion kit for any vehicle. However, there are very few vehicles that have EPA certified conversion kits available. We currently have no EPA certified conversion kit for your vehicle. If the kit is not EPA certified, then it would not be legal for us to do the conversion. If we break this law, we are subject to a $10,000 a day EPA fine per vehicle that we convert. In order to gain EPA certification, complex emissions testing need to be done on the vehicle using dynamometers. Dynamometers run vehicles on computer simulated, federally regulated drive tracks to test emissions. After sending this info to the EPA, they may grant a certificate of conformity for that vehicle. This process costs a substantial amount of money per vehicle engine platform (approximately $50,000). The EPA certification is not for a vehicle, per se, but for that vehicle's engine platform # (aka Engine Family #, or Engine test group #). The engine platform number corresponds to only certain vehicles. I have an EPA certification for a 2008 Ford Focus with an engine platform # 8FMXV02.0VD4. What this translates into in lay terms is that I have a certification for about 60% of the 2008 Ford Focus's. Generally speaking engine platform numbers can change from year to year of a vehicle, so I do not have a certification for any other year of Ford Focus. If one gains this certification it expires December 31 of that year, regardless of when the cert was issued. In other words, the certs are not necessarily good for an entire year, as one may occasionally obtain the certs mid-year. In order to maintain the certification one has to resubmit the same exact data to the EPA for a charge of $10,000. We don't have to run the tests again, we simply re-send them the same exact data. This fee would be applied every single year that one wanted to keep that certification. So, for instance, to certify a 2008 Ford Focus we need to spend an extremely large amount of money to begin with and then $10,000 every year that we would want to maintain that certification. This certification is for the kit itself and the kit corresponds to a vehicle with a particular engine platform #. Feel free to continue to research this process, but I can assure you that you will not be able to find an EPA certified conversion kit for a vehicle that I have not listed. The only other certification that the EPA recognizes is certifications through the California Air Resources Board (CARB). CARB is much stricter than the EPA. If a vehicle is not on the list I have included, you can find a kit, and perhaps someone willing to do the installation, but you would be breaking the law and would be subject to the EPA fines if you were caught. The EPA considers the installation of a non-certified conversion kit "tampering with a federally approved emission control system." I have the unfortunate task of having to explain this to about 30 people a day. It really doesn't make me happy to be turning away business, and not be legally allowed to convert a vehicle to an environmentally friendly, domestically-produced, economically viable fuel. I have included some vital information to assist you in your quest as I want to help you. Please be advised that any information you may receive to the contrary of what I have just explained will be incorrect. If you already have or are willing to purchase these listed vehicles, we would be happy to do a conversion. Our business typically does conversions for trucking fleets that make certain to purchase the right vehicles before we begin the conversion process. If you have or can acquire one of the vehicles I have listed, then we can do a conversion for about $10,000. Please understand that the EPA certification costs are substantial, and the technological costs are substantial, so we cannot do a conversion for less than this without losing money in the process. It is generally more economically viable for a fleet, hence our limited conversions on individual vehicles. We are using top of the line equipment that interfaces with modern, computer-controlled vehicle technology. Many other CNG kits that may be found on-line for cheaper prices are illegal and bypass the computer emission control systems in vehicles, rather than interfacing with the computer controls. The problem with these kits is that "OBDII" (your computer controls) is designed to understand when something is wrong with your vehicle. If your kit bypasses your OBDII sensors it can be potentially very dangerous for your vehicle and may cause your catalytic converter to burn up, as OBDII regulates the amount of fuel that is sent to your catalytic converter. Please be wary of on-line CNG kit sellers. I highly recommend against a CNG kit that does not interface with OBDII. It is not impossible to find an OBDII interfacing CNG kit that would work for your vehicle, but we cannot risk the substantial EPA fines. I apologize that it is more difficult than it rightfully should be. We are currently lobbying with the EPA to change the legalities, but in the meantime we can only convert the listed vehicles.[25]

Indeed, most fleet owners first purchase a gasoline-burning car or truck new and have the factory or dealer deliver it directly to the conversion house first where it is upfitted before the customer ever receives the vehicle.[26] In other words, the factories first build the vehicles wrong, and then the customer arranges for them to be converted to the right system.

Despite the risk, an upfitting underground has developed. Utah has become an underground epicenter for illegal CNG conversions. CNG sells for the equivalent of $.85 per gallon there. The Internet is filled with chatter about Utah residents desiring and offering uncertified upfits using Italian and Argentinean conversion kits not approved by the EPA. In many cases, the names of specifics vendors or products are blocked by automotive website moderators.[27]

A sample June 28, 2008 post on one automotive website stated: "It seems Utah has a state run program to encourage conversion to compressed natural gas. Based on a quick scan, 'illegal' conversions cost around $3000 installed ($1500 for the kit, $1500 for installation). They won't meet 'EPA certification standards,' so you will have trouble getting past a smog inspection. Additionally, it is a federal crime to tamper with your car's emission system, so these converters make you a criminal should your conversion go into a car built after around 1996 (start OBDII)." Getting EPA certified systems seems to cost a lot more: $8000 to $18,000. It isn't clear that the 'EPA approved' kits are any better in mechanical terms. Anyway, the legal issues are avoided by sticking with older cars.... The EPA searches the internet for people bragging about their illegal conversions."[28]

In other words, Americans desperate to get off oil and switch to CNG must hide in the shadows to make it affordable. The government has criminalized much of the ad hoc upfitting underway as of summer 2008. Neiburger says, "I think there is a certain legitimacy to EPA's position. If a conversion is not done correctly, it can make emissions worse. But in other industrialized countries where they have the highest emission standards, the government there just certifies the company—and not each and every engine." He adds, "It is not possible to function under these circumstances. If only we could get certified for our company and not each engine. There must be a middle ground."[29]

One CNG retrofitting expert who must work with the government hourly said, "Look, if we hit an oil crisis, we are screwed. The EPA is the biggest impediment." An electric upfitting engineer stated, "If we need to retrofit on a mass scale, we are S.O.L."[30]

The feeling among numerous oil crisis experts is that in the event of an oil supply emergency, EPA standards will have to be suspended. There is ample precedent. All federal environmental, occupational and other regulatory standards were suspended by government decision to enable the fast construction of the Alaska pipeline after the 1973 Arab Oil Embargo. In a similar move, municipal and county governmental style powers were conveyed by the state of Florida upon the developers of Disneyworld in Orlando in the sixties to facilitate that important project. The Manhattan Project to build an atomic bomb was also freed of all environmental and bureaucratic encumbrances.[31]

EPA officials—under pressure for mismanagement, and facing widespread accusations by media and public action groups for being pawns of polluters and covering up global warming reports with censored science, declined to answer questions directly or even discuss the matter of upfitting. Officials did however email a ready statement: "Our rigorous certification requirements are in place to protect public health and the environment. While these products may be designed with good intentions, they could actually end up harming public health, the environment and damaging vehicles. By law, we are obligated to evaluate these products." One upfitting engineer stated, "The EPA is our biggest problem." Neiburger scoffed, "We need action. Every time I try to tell someone what is happening in this country, they just don't believe me." He added, "Do you have any idea how scared a politician is to mess with the Clean Air Act?"[32]

A crash program of retrofitting would not only help free the country of dependence on oil, and save the country from collapse in the event of a true protracted oil interruption, but also quickly lead to a dramatic clean-up in air pollution. If oil is substantially interrupted, EPA standards and enforcement will have to be suspended to help the nation get off oil—with the same alacrity marshaled to enable the Alaska pipeline thereby helping us remain on oil. After all, the most EPA-certified and qualified vehicles in America—including Hummers, Escalades, and Honda Pilots, are the ones causing all the pollution and ensuring our addiction to oil.

Yet it would be an oversimplification to believe that if the EPA or CARB suddenly suspended its enforcement, upfitters could move swiftly to correct America's woes. If upfitters received a green light they would need everything.

Retrofitting is not in its infancy in America—it is prenatal. Although there are numerous options for conversion to alternative propulsion systems and fuels, there is almost no one available to undertake a large scale fix.

Upfitting *en masse* requires massive numbers of conversion kits, gas storage tanks, batteries, and electronic controls. These do not exist at hand. Crash production and acquisition of components would be required. Shortages would be a constant worry. Installers and technicians would need to be found and trained. Most importantly, standards would have to be rapidly adopted so upfitting issues at one center could be addressed at another center. All this could take six to twelve months at breakneck speed. If the expansion of upfitting is begun before the crisis, it can be more organized and successful. If it grows up in an overnight upheaval because of a sudden oil stoppage, the process will be haphazard. That may happen.

After the upfitting community mushrooms to the dimension needed to tackle the challenge, an entire service infrastructure will need to be developed. Today, internal combustion machines can be serviced virtually everywhere from the smallest and dustiest town to the biggest cosmopolitan city. Once cars begin converting to electric, CNG, flex-fuel or any other alternative, who will service them? A complete service sector will need to spring up. Skilled mechanics trained in diagnosing, servicing, repairing and replacing sophisticated electronics, alt fuel systems, battery defects, and a myriad of other issues will need to appear. Those service centers will require spare parts: hoses, seals, tanks, batteries, engines, black boxes—just as they now do for ordinary cars. The availability of service will probably dictate the type of conversion a vehicle undergoes.

Because no fuel or propulsion alternative will be king, there will likely to be pockets of upfit popularity. Utah, California and Texas will certainly be epicenters for CNG. California also will undoubtedly be a center for electric. Ammonia fuel would be sensible in the nation's agricultural heartland because a distribution system already exists. Alcohol fuels and second-generation biofuels will undoubtedly share facilities everywhere. Just as people today require an authorized or qualified service center for their Honda, Lexus or Ford, so too, alt fuel upfitting will factor in the convenient availability of service.

After the upfitting industry has rushed into larger quarters, trained a battalion of technicians, obtained a sure supply of components, settled on standards and helped seed a service sector, one additional factor remains: the fuel.

Driving a CNG car requires access to natural gas and refueling appliances. Electric vehicles need standard outlets. Those two appear easy. Fuel supplies will be more questionable in the case of alcohol fuels, ammonia, hydrogen, recycled vegetable oils and so forth.

In other words, once the car has been upfitted, where does it find alternative fuel? This is the point where most car and truck makers that are deliberately going slow on alternative vehicles, such as Honda and GM, invoke the magic word: "infrastructure." By this, auto execs mean gas stations with dispensers. "Lack of infrastructure" claims are the surest way to know the automakers are consciously going slow on alternative fuels and propulsion. The response to such arguments is "home refueling" or "neighborhood refueling."

Of course, the newest electric cars will probably only need a standard plug. Electric cars will increasingly make gasoline stations—and gasoline—vastly less necessary. When electric cars ruled the road—or the rutted unpaved byways that passed for roads—at the beginning of the 20th century, there were no gas stations. The notion of home generation of electricity was the idea of the day. Indeed General Electric invented the "Electrant," that is, the electric hydrant, for city streets in 1911. The Electrant was a device resembling a parking meter which recharged the battery of a vehicle parked near it. But electric cars were subverted by a combination of corrupt forces, and by 1914, internal combustion was crowned king. Claims that an armada of electric cars would strain the grid have been repeatedly dismissed by utilities. In fact, as recently as July 23, 2008, the Electric Power Research Institute issued press statements reiterating that it could accommodate the first expected wave of electric cars in 2010 as easily as it has managed the sudden mass adoption of plasma TV screens.[33] The expected onset of more wind farms, geothermal plants, nuclear reactors, and other non-greenhouse sources of generation, including home generation via small scale wind turbines, make electric a leading choice.

Nothing will be as universally available as electric. But CNG would be close, especially as a bridge technology. CNG can be dispensed from a home appliance not much bigger than a small lectern. Fuelmaker is the chief manufacturer of those home refueling devices, aptly called "Phill." Honda, which makes the CNG car to be paired with the home refueling Phill unit, is the controlling shareholder of Fuelmaker and has worked arduously to keep Fuelmaker Phill units out of most states that want them. Similarly, Honda refuses to sell its own highly touted CNG Civics to most Americans who want them, focusing instead on a few markets in several states, mainly in California and New York. Honda claims that for all intents and purposes it can only sell the cars where CNG gas stations exist, which is the opposite of the advantage of its own Phill system. But people have begun purchasing alternative dispensers. Some versions of the fueler can fill multiple cars, making shared appliances or fleet appliances a good idea. Indeed, some Phill dealers, such as in Utah, sell CNG dispensers to those driving not just Hondas but also homegrown conversions.[34] Eventually, the carmakers will have to unlock the distribution of the handy appliances which make gas stations unnecessary or the natural gas utilities will do so.

The availability of more exotic fuels such as Brazilian ethanol, methanol, trash-to-gas blends, coal-to-methanol blends, recycled fats and so forth will be a localized phenomenon at first and then expand regionally until availability resembles a national network. That will work perfectly for local fleets such as taxis, delivery trucks and cars intended for localized sales. Indeed Honda now sells or leases hydrogen cars and CNG cars for localized markets. Numerous McDonald's franchisees across America run their vehicles on diesel made locally from their own recycled french fry oil. A company called RTI collects used fats and oils from approximately 7,500 McDonald's restaurants in the U.S.—more than half its total outlets. About 80 percent of that throwaway frying oil is recycled into biodiesel.[35]

Home sugar ethanol stills and dispensers are being sold by a California start-up called E-Fuel. The firm is so swamped with inquiries that it will not even list its phone number on its website. It takes the firm ten days to respond to dealer applications. E-Fuel's Microfueler dispenser will be supported by its growing dealer network that will fill the fueler with a sugar ethanol mix—or you can brew it yourself to EPA standards by combining 13 pounds of ordinary sugar with yeast and water in the controlled Microfueler environment to produce one gallon of ethanol. The system can yield 35 gallons per week from 470 pounds of sugar. This is more than adequate for at least one commuting car or neighborhood runabout, and perhaps two such vehicles.

E-Fuel does not use ordinary household sugar. Table sugar is too expensive at about 50 cents per pound. The sugar will be either surplus or unfit for human consumption. But recent legislation has reduced the cost of sugar-to-ethanol surplus supply to about 2 cents per pound. Inedible sugar can also be purchased at a similar price from Mexico under NAFTA. E-Fuel estimates that Micro-Fueler owners will be able to make ethanol for approximately $1 per gallon, and possibly pennies per gallon if used restaurant and bar alcohols are recycled. E-Fuel, at press time, was establishing relationships with major sugar distributors to supply the requisite yeast-enriched sugar blend to its dealers or directly to MicroFueler owners. The $10,000 machine cost is almost 50 percent offset by various tax credits and incentives, the company states.[36]

Infrastructure is not needed—ingenuity is.

A national will is needed. Ironically, hostile Iran, one of the globe's largest oil suppliers and a potential swing factor in any global petroleum stoppage, is the second largest gasoline importer in the world. Having no refineries, Iran must import gasoline and other finished petroleum products to operate its national life and military sector. Starting in 2007, Western sanctions slowly began drying up international trading partners. One by one, suppliers terminated their trading relationships. Iran, awash in oil, feared it might have no gasoline. Therefore, it embarked on a massive national program to convert 20 percent of its fleet per year to CNG. Iran enjoys abundant reserves of natural gas. The cheap one-day CNG conversions are fast and effective. More than 100 conversion centers through Iran charge a subsidized fee equal to about $50. Iran added about a half million CNG cars from June, 2007, to June, 2008.[37]

A retrofitting revolution will be needed to boost America off oil. Where will the manpower come from? Where will it occur? Who will pay for it?

Marching among the first ranks of the retrofitting revolution will be established Qualified Vehicle Manufacturers, the so-called

QVMs. These are factory-approved craftsman designated by manufacturers to convert their standard issue cars into stretch limos, ambulances, hearses and other specialty transportation. There are scores of QVMs around the country. No one knows how to slice up, reassemble and make over a vehicle like they do.

One of the biggest QVMs in America is Empire Coachworks International of East Brunswick, NJ. Empire is responsible for creating the gigantic stretch Hummers, Town Cars, Escalades, and other elongated limousines that stand as the seeming paragon of conspicuous gas consumption. Empire's CEO Michael Misseri was asked about the gas consumption he enables. "I am against petroleum," he declares, adding "We can't just sit back any more and let this petroleum problem kill us. All cars should be CNG." Empire is already working with the city of New York on a 1,000-car test project to convert city fleets to CNG. He would like to upfit thousands more to CNG. "I need protection from CARB and EPA," he says. As of summer 2008, he was going through the paperwork to obtain legitimate certification. Asked if he was ready to "step up to the plate" to help retrofit America, Misseri snapped, "I am already at the plate. I have an 88,000 square foot facility and I am ready."

In any retrofitting revolution, Misseri will be among the first forces. Who else will join the ranks? The underground upfitters waiting to step out of the shadows, custom shops, ordinary auto dealers trying to recapture income lost when the nation bolted from fuel inefficient SUVs and other gas guzzlers. The "war footing" so many have called for should come to pass as military and National Guard motor pools establish outreach upfit services. Corporate and government fleet services will have to join. The Postal Service, Wal-Mart, and other major fleet operators will be a lynchpin. Automotive schools, such as the one operated by Spokane Community College, have expressed a keen desire to join the movement.

Just behind the first responders will be a second massive wave of retrofitters. These additional hundreds of thousands will come from the ranks of autoworkers cast off by the rapidly contracting auto industry which has closed numerous plants for weeks at a time and sometimes permanently. This legion of ready automotive workers who have been told their jobs are gone, their futures are uncertain, and that the nation's mobility is imperiled will gladly apply their skills to help rescue the cars they built.

The mighty computer industry began with hobbyists tinkering in their basements and garages. Within a short number of years, they came to rule the world. Upfitting has a model to emulate.

Revolution, they say, is required to overturn the established order when it no longer serves the greater good. A retrofitting revolution is long overdue. Without it, all the conservation and new behavior Americans can muster to comply with *The Plan* or their own economic imperatives will be for naught. The sooner the retrofitting revolutionaries pour out of their garages and march down the street to the town square, the faster any plan can be implemented.

This will cost billions. So the questions arise: how will it be paid or who will pay for it? That one is easy.

CHAPTER SIX

Week Five— Funding the Fix

It will cost billions and take years to undo a century of oil addiction. Instituting *The Plan* and retrofitting America will be a long, tortuous process of upheaval. Demand restrictions and fuel switching should commence in the first week of an oil crisis. A retrofitting revolution should commence by the third week of that crisis.

The national upfit may begin three weeks into the crisis, but it will take months to show real progress, and then years of arduous work to wrest the country from its oil addiction. Those years will be very expensive.

Individual vehicle conversions can cost between $5,000 and $20,000. Large fleet upfits will cost millions of dollars. Retrofitting will require a nationwide private sector mobilization of manpower, components and training, costing billions. Public transit will require millions upon millions to defray fare box shortfalls should it open its doors to masses of commuters at free and/or deep-discount fares.

Where will the money come from? Numerous sources rise to the forefront for consideration. The first and most obvious source of funding is the immediate adjustment of Congressional incentives, subsidies and barriers. American taxpayers have directly and indirectly paid billions of dollars to reward and prolong the oil addiction. The list is long and discouraging. During elections, candidates speak the right words, but then vote against the national need. Priorities need to be changed.

For example, more than $8 billion in annual federal subsidies have been handed to oil companies to give Big Oil an "incentive to drill." Additional subsidies of almost $2 billion per year have been granted to oil companies to compensate them for blending corn ethanol. Yet oil company revenues have stunned the world with the greatest accretion of profits in the history of mankind. In 2005, one oil company alone, ExxonMobil, logged a string of stunning record quarterly profits. ExxonMobil's third quarter results in 2005, after Hurricane Katrina wiped out Gulf Coast facilities, yielded $9.9 billion. That was a three-month record. Fourth quarter 2005 profits rose to $10.7 billion, again a record. Just one second of ExxonMobil's 2005 profit—$1,146—could purchase enough gasoline for the average car to drive almost 10,300 miles that year. Exxon profits continued their updraft.[1]

In August 2008, Exxon announced an $11.68 billion second quarter profit. These dollars are not income—but profit. Quarterly profits for ExxonMobil alone for the rest of this century's first decade are predicted to continue to exceed the earnings of all non-oil Fortune 500 companies combined. ExxonMobil is just one of the oil companies that have recorded astronomical earnings. In 2007, the oil industry recorded revenues of approximately $1.9 trillion, more than three-quarters of which went to the five major integrated oil companies. Profits for the industry totaled over $155 billion, with those same five major companies garnering three-quarters of it.[2] Yet decamillions in tax money continue to support their enterprise.

The so-called "Hummer tax loophole" that granted tax credits and deductions almost equivalent to the purchase price of the largest and heaviest SUVs, has been estimated to have cost taxpayers between $840 million and $987 million for every 100,000 of the 50 or so qualifying models. The total taxpayer losses arising from the Hummer loophole as of summer 2008 have not yet been fully calculated, but they are a staggering multibillion dollar amount.

Moreover, the tax credit structure for hybrid vehicles has now been turned upside down. Credits for the most fuel efficient cars, such as the Toyota Prius and Honda Civic, have been phased out, while big gas guzzling hybrid SUVs, such as the GM Tahoe which achieves just 20 MPG, earn full credit.[3] These measures were not White House dicta, they arose from Congressional votes.

Just the few taxation examples cited here amount to more than $11 billion per year in federal outlays. These have been flowing year after year. A careful examination might find scores billions of dollars annually spent to support oil consumption. One recent study of tax incentives and government programs supporting oil estimated at least $38 billion and perhaps as much as $114.6 billion annually.[4] Indeed, a half-trillion dollars in oil subsidies and incentives may have already been expended just in the years since the September 11 attacks when our country was to redouble its efforts at energy independence.

In addition to readjusting existing tax-based oil supports, the country would save enormous federal expenditures by reducing dependence on oil. The nation has spent $7 trillion on foreign oil from 1979 to 2000. Estimates of America's 2008 expenditures for foreign oil range from $700 billion to $1 trillion.[5]

The true price of every gallon of gasoline, adding in expenditures for tax subsidies and government programs, harm to our health as a result of toxic emissions, environmental damage and military operations to protect the supply, is almost impossible to reliably calculate. The range of estimates of "external costs" is so dramatic it becomes an exercise in fuzzy mathematics. It is like counting stars. We know they are out there but can only guess at the astronomical figure.

But some of the most quoted and informed studies conclude the true cost of oil to be more than $15 per gallon, creating a yearly national pump-supporting expenditure of between $231 billion and $1 trillion. The numbers defy hardening because military costs—amounting to more than $6 billion per month in Iraq—require a political measuring stick to attribute them to oil. However, this much is known about external costs: they are real and they are massive. The Defense Department allocates from $55 billion to $96.3 billion annually to safeguard petroleum supplies, two-thirds of which are pumped from the Persian Gulf. Social, health and environmental programs add staggering sums, but segregating how much of those expenditures are rooted in petroleum is impossible, even though most experts agree the expenses are significant.[6]

Oil has escaped a true financial accounting. Beyond mere cash expenditures, the human toll of death and dismemberment arising from America's necessary protective military presence in the Middle East as well as the harm done to the health of its citizens is incalculable. Family anguish is not measured in joules, but in jolts—not in dollars, but in devastation.

Meanwhile, since 2003, OPEC and its members have spent some $13.3 million on federal lobbying, about half of which comes from Saudi Arabia. Since 2003, oil companies have spent $59.4 million supporting the price of oil and our dependence on it.[7]

Special governmental expenditures will be in order to fund the fix, based on savings or reallocated dollars. The precedents are numerous. In the first weeks of 2008, an extreme economic downturn—much of it related to escalating oil prices—prompted an immediate decision by Washington to undertake a major cash giveaway. The result was a $168 billion so-called "economic stimulus package." Checks of $600 per taxpayer were mass mailed to millions of households in June 2008. The checks were designed to spur consumer spending on "things," that is, material goods and services. It was thought that the cash would ignite a flurry of purchases of plasma TVs, clothing and other discretionary items, as opposed to simple savings or catch-up economics. But the mass handout did little to spur the economy.[8] Most people used the money to keep up with the rising cost of food, energy, and the general cost of living.

During the 2008 presidential campaign, Democratic nominee Barack Obama suggested a $1,000 per family cash payout to assist with high energy bills.[9]

In 2006, Congress voted to spend $900 million plus $100 million on administrative expenses to send two $40 coupons to every requesting household for a special upfitting program. This federal billion was supported by an additional $1 billion mobilized by a private industry educational initiative. What was the upfit? Was it to become more energy efficient? No, it was to upgrade to digital TV converter boxes.[10]

The infamous "Bridge to Nowhere," connecting an Alaskan island of 50 inhabitants to shorten their 15-minute ferry wait, received $325 million in Congressional funding in 2005, which was later revoked due to public uproar. The 3.5 mile Big Dig tunnel in Boston was constructed at a cost of more than $6 billion per mile and as of summer 2008 the tab has exceeded $22 billion and continues to grow.[11] The federal government's ability to generate multibillion dollar expenditures is seemingly limitless.

At the end of the day, America will also have to ask itself how much damage the economy sustained as a result of the addiction to oil. A similar question had been asked of the toxic waste industry when the Superfund was created in 1980. The federal government established a list of about 100 "potentially responsible parties" and they were singly and collectively obligated to pay hundreds of millions in clean-up costs. In 1998 and 1999 alone, the responsible parties paid in some $328 million.[12]

The Exxon Valdez disaster cost Exxon more than $1 billion in damages, reimbursements and other compensatory programs. The tobacco industry, in a settlement with 46 states, was assessed $206 billion and became obligated to fund a spectrum of ameliorating programs, such as anti-smoking projects. In the tobacco case, it was argued that everyone in America knew cigarettes were dangerous because of the omnipresent Surgeon General's warnings and anti-smoking campaigns.[13]

In June 2008, an aviation pioneer and profiteer no less stellar than Virgin Group chairman Richard Branson told the Global Humanitarian Forum on Climate Change that aviation is "a dirty business" and that airlines should be willing to pay for the damage they cause to the environment. Indeed, said Branson, he was willing to pay carbon-emissions taxes on his own aviation business, Virgin Air. "If you run a dirty business— an airline business, a shipping business... coal business, you should pay for the privilege because you are doing damage," said Branson.[14]

Clearly, America must mend its addiction to oil, recover damages, defray the cost of upfitting and make a statement about the conscious corporate actions undertaken at the expense of society and the planet. The damage to the environment, to the nation's health, to global warming, and to the economy could be incalculable. The transgression trebles because automobiles never needed to be on oil in the first place. Who is to blame? Is it the exporters? Is it Big Oil?

It would be easy to blame Arab nations and other OPEC countries. But in truth, their oil industries sprang up only after Western oil imperialists invaded their territory after World War I to create oil states with imposed puppet governments to ensure a cheap, abundant supply. The citizens of those countries hated the foreign presence and by the end of World War II had turned the tables upon the West. By September 2001, they began extracting prodigious damages—political and economic.[15] The West knew the volatile cultural and geopolitical territory before they decided to make their modern societies dependent upon the black substance beneath the sands of the Mideast and then transport it around the world, too frequently over the bodies of their dead soldiers. Even so, the exporters certainly bear culpability to a degree.

It would be easy to blame Big Oil. The oil companies have used America's vulnerability to enrich their coffers at tornadic rates. They have used their political muscle to maintain multibillion dollar tax breaks and prolong favorable governmental relations. Moreover, Big Oil has declined to develop the alternatives needed to break America and the world from an addiction that is making industrialized society more vulnerable every day. Often, these companies have used patent sequestration and go-slow development strategies to ensure that solar, electric and other alt fuels come online but only gradually. The energy status quo, one of glacial incrementalism, guarantees that the world will drink petroleum until the last unaffordable drop—and only then switch. The longer Big Oil holds out, the scarcer and more costly its commodity becomes. Big Oil also bears culpability.

But who exercised the greatest historic role in America's oil addiction? Who was the pivotal culprit?

When the automobile was invented in 1835, it was an electric vehicle. Until the first years of the 20th century, nearly all fleets and individual automobiles were electric. Henry Ford and Thomas Edison combined their millions and their talents to create an electric car network. It was only industrial sabotage and manipulation by the emerging auto industry in the pre-World War I years that subverted the forgotten Ford-Edison project and the electric car generally, in favor of internal combustion machines.[16]

Oil played a major role in World War I, in the post-war period, then again in World War II, and in the reconstructive years after that.[17]

After the Arab Oil Embargo of 1973, the warning shot heard around the world may have been fired in the Middle East, but the echoes reverberated loudest in Detroit. Without Detroit, the rapacious desires of the exporters and oil companies would have been unfulfilled. Expensive oil requires an eager guzzler. During the three decades plus since the 1973 crisis, major carmakers have deliberately foisted increasingly dangerous and defective automobiles upon the American public. Most people associate Detroit's "dangerous cars" and "defective cars" with the famous exploding gas tanks, the rollovers of unstable vehicles, engine systems that self-ignite, "lemon engines," and the cavalcade of mechanical recalls that Detroit has become known for.

Less debated is the role car companies played in consciously making defective and dangerous vehicles that poisoned the air with carcinogenic emissions. Moreover, most people have not brought to the forefront one of the greatest defects: "the reverse leak." Automobiles were designed to be so heavy and inefficient that they over-consumed oil. They did not leak—they did the opposite—they guzzled. Had Detroit made a device that consumed too much electricity, made too much noise, vibrated too much, burned too much engine lubricant or was similarly inefficient, dropped rubber on the streets, it would have been a flagged problem. Knowing the country was in an oil crisis, Detroit made millions of cars that would make the situation worse. Moreover, by selling the same low mileage cars to Mexico, Pakistan, Russia, India and China, they magnified the problem for every American. The more SUVs GM and Ford sold to China and India, the more expensive oil became for all in the world. Oil is globally fungible—and so is the effect of gas guzzling. Detroit certainly bears pivotal culpability.

Like those who bought and smoked cigarettes of their own free will despite years of luminous warnings, it would be hard not to identify the unindicted co-conspirator: the public. But, at the same time, alternative fuel vehicles were not available, including electric cars. When clean electric cars did exist, the car manufacturers—led by GM—embarked upon a now infamous campaign to physically destroy them in giant crushing machines.

When such clean vehicles as the compressed natural gas-powered Honda Civic GX were rolled out, Honda staunchly refused to sell them to most who wanted the cars, and for those who could purchase the car, they made it painfully difficult. Honda sold approximately 138,000 vehicles in July, 2008; it deliberately manufactured approximately 90 CNG cars that month, according to company sources and sales data. The GX became useful as a "storefront" trophy that the Japanese company could advertise in America as positive public relations.[18] But Honda feared the innovation that would drive business away from their low-mileage SUVs.

GREEN FLEET SUPERFUND

Tobacconizing oil means taking a tobacco approach to the companies that ensured America's addiction to oil. The companies responsible for that addiction should be assessed, with the monies going into a Green Fleet Superfund, akin to the toxic waste Superfund. The Superfund would help finance conversions, alt fuel start-ups and other fixes. There could be numerous measuring sticks for assessing the financial liability of carmakers, but perhaps the fairest one might be to examine their cumulative annual fleet mileage since 1973.

In the tobacco experience, consumers were also assessed. They paid and continue to pay enormous punitive taxes for every pack of cigarettes purchased—one of the so-called "sin taxes." The Green

Fleet Superfund would do likewise. The infrastructure is already there. The Energy Tax Act of 1978 established a so-called "Gas Guzzler Tax" on the sale of new vehicles with fuel economy rated less than 22.5 MPG. The IRS collects the fees, ranging from $1,000 for a vehicle under 22 MPG to $7,700 for a vehicle rated less than 12.5 MPG. A government website explains, "The purpose of the Gas Guzzler Tax is to discourage the production and purchase of fuel inefficient vehicles." However, in typical governmental fashion, the tax inexplicably exempts SUVs, minivans, and similar gas guzzlers. Hence, the fee is reserved for just a few models, mainly luxury imports such as the Rolls Royce, the Bentley, and the notoriously oil consuming Lamborghini.[19]

MAKE THE GAS GUZZLER TAX WORK

A true gas guzzler tax should actually include the genuine gas guzzlers such as GM Hummers, Cadillac Escalades, Ford Navigators, and Honda Pilots—all among the worst mileage vehicles operating in the country. Moreover, the tax should apply not just to new cars, but to all cars currently on the road. The tax should be re-assessed annually in some form until the car is upfitted.

Gas guzzler revenues should be earmarked for the Green Fleet Superfund, and each individual should be able to draw on a significant portion of their own assessment to undertake upfitting if done in a timely fashion.

UPFIT LOANS

The Green Fleet Superfund would be augmented by an entirely new and vibrant segment of the financial services industry: upfit loans. Just as people are accustomed to student loans, home improvement loans, car loans, disaster loans, and reconstruction loans—some of which are government guaranteed and amortized over years, the new Upfit Finance sector would help individuals and commercial fleets convert to alternative fuels and alternative forms of propulsion.

TAX CREDITS

Tax credits and incentives—the same type extended to beneficiaries of the Hummer Loophole—would be available to those moving to green vehicles or green fleets.

WINDFALL PROFITS TAX

A windfall profits tax on oil companies springs to the mind of many. Every attempt to impose a windfall profits tax has been miserably botched by the federal government or other administrators. So has alternative fuel development. That doesn't mean that either is inappropriate. Indeed, the very terms "windfall profits" and "excise tax" hark back to the concept of excess energy profits. It goes back to the 18th century, when wood was a dominant source of energy in England and its American colonies. All wood was carefully controlled by the king. Colonists were not allowed to use lumber wider than one foot unless through an act of God, such as a windstorm blowing a limb down on one's property. Only then could one sell more wood than expected and reap greater profits, called fittingly enough "windfall profits." This excess profit was taxed and some believe that excess became the basis for the term "excise." Others disagree, including Samuel Johnson, who defined "excise tax" as "a hateful tax levied on commodities, and adjudged not by the common judges of property, but wretches hired by those to whom excise is paid."[20]

Samuel Johnson notwithstanding, special taxes on extravagant profits by any name have often been imposed. Four "excess profit taxes" were legislated during World War II and again during the Korean War. In 1980, a poorly administered windfall profits tax was imposed on the oil industry. In Chicago, since regulations for taxi fare increases were tied to profits, the cab companies artificially inflated expenses to pretend they had not exceeded their profit limits.[21] A Superfund assessment on polluters is just a tax in the guise of a penalty.

Hence, if oil company windfall profits could be earmarked for the Green Fleet Superfund, it would rectify an imbalance in society so great that it calls out for correction.

JOB CREATION

Far from being an expense, the Green Fleet Superfund will create a massive new automotive sector, with hundreds of thousands of jobs located in every community. The technology will be exportable and deliver America a new global niche akin to the primacy it achieved in computers. In the end, we will have cast off a 19th century propulsion system in favor of one that is environmentally renewable, ecologically sustainable, economically affordable, and petropolitically rational.

The Green Fleet Superfund would combine with other government funding to help finance a genuine Manhattan Project for getting off oil. It would help speed an upfitting industry, the crash development and expansion of alternative fuels, upfit training, mass transit, mini transit, funding for new green fleets, and the purchase of these new green vehicles.

Indeed a Manhattan Project is long overdue.

Just how expensive was the Manhattan Project? Total expenditures for the original Manhattan Project were about $1.89 billion in World War II dollars spent over four years. That sum included slightly more than $512 million for the key Gaseous Diffusion Plant and $477.6 million for the Electromagnetic Plant so indispensable to fission. Actual research and development, however, clocked in at only $69.6 million. The World War II total of $1.89 billion equals about $20 billion in 2008 dollars.[22]

By way of perspective, during World War II and the Manhattan Project years, America spent much more on other weaponry—the 1996 equivalent of $31.5 billion on ordinary bombs, mines and grenades, $24 billion on small arms, and $64 billion on tanks.[23]

How realistic is an expenditure of $20 billion today to develop independence by means of alternative fuels? Answer: It simply requires national will and a national priority. Examples abound.

The Apollo program to land a man on the moon totaled nearly

$20 billion, or about $135 billion in 2008 dollars. Each of the rocket programs alone, such as the Saturn program, cost between $28 and $45 billion in 2008 dollars—both more than a Manhattan Project. The Hong Kong Airport, which required the frenetic creation and deconstruction of several islands, opened in 1998 at a cost $19.9 billion. The Chunnel under the English Channel cost an estimated $15 billion in the 1990s. The Trans-Alaska Pipeline, which was rushed into construction after the first Arab oil shock in 1973, cost nearly $9 billion at the time, which equals about $45 billion in 2008 money. The Taishet-Nakhodka Pipeline, now under way, will carry natural gas from Siberia to northwest China over a tortuous 2,581-mile course at a projected cost of between $15 and $18 billion. Another just-announced natural gas pipeline, this one from Alaska to the lower Forty-Eight under the aegis of ExxonMobil, BP and ConocoPhillips, will require between $25 and $30 billion. The Trans Texas Corridor, a newly planned network of some 4,000 miles of intermodal highways spanning Texas, will cost $31.4 million per centerline mile or an estimated total of about $145.4 billion to $183.5 billion—give or take a few billion. Boston's infamous Big Dig cost more than $22 billion for a 3.5-mile stretch—or a Manhattan Project-sized roadway to enable a few-minute drive.[24]

Some deep water oil drilling in the Gulf of Mexico requires as much as a $5 billion investment. ExxonMobil alone could fund its own Manhattan Project with two to three months of its 2008 hyperprofit.

The war in Iraq cost is estimated by some to cost about $100 billion annually, or a Manhattan Project-sized enterprise every two months.[25]

Since the United States dropped two atomic bombs on Japan in August 1945, this country has been willing to undertake great enterprises like the Manhattan Project on a regular basis. Our nation has not been shy about spending large sums. If energy-starved partners in Europe and Asia were included in the finances, $20 billion over four years—the Manhattan Project budget—would emerge as a rather unspectacular sum, especially if split among the top ten industrialized nations. Indeed, all industrial nations have a vested interest in sharing clean, renewable energy to wean the world off of oil.[26]

But we cannot fix this problem by simply throwing money at it. We cannot intelligently mobilize to repair the damage without permanently kicking our addiction to oil. Is there any true fix?

There is.

CHAPTER SEVEN

Week Seven—
The True Fix

For decades, the major U.S. carmakers have refused to sell America cars that were fuel efficient. Otherwise, the vehicles were perfect, tantalizing all human senses. Ice making, butt warming, ear booming, back adjusting, video entertaining, rear camera viewing, night visioning, Bluetooth broadcasting, GPS mapping, the latest cars and trucks have represented marvelous feats of automotive engineering. But these magnificent machines have always featured one prominent defect. The carmakers claimed they could not make them fuel efficient.

Now America and the world must see the truth, repair the damage and take drastic action in the event of a true oil crisis. However, despite all the demand restraint society can launch within the first seven days of an oil crisis, despite all the retrofitting the nation can muster by the third week, despite all the economic contortions to create a Green Fleet Superfund in the fifth week of such a crisis, *The Plan* is doomed to failure unless it becomes the centerpiece of a radiating long-term fix.

The American car and truck industry sells approximately 15 to 17 million vehicles annually. Car manufacturers maintain that sales level even in a bad year, such as 2008, which saw sales at the low end of the range. Vehicles just wear out and must be replaced within 9 to 11 years, the so-called "scrappage point." Good year or bad year, by any measure, Detroit sells more than a million oil-drinking cars and trucks per month. The nation would be hard-pressed, at least in the first months, to upfit a million vehicles per month—or about 5,000 per day—just to keep up with Detroit.

In other words, society cannot fix the problem faster than Detroit can make it worse. Every gas guzzler Detroit manages to sell ensures that its owner—and society—will be dependent upon petroleum for a decade to come. Imagine what the political and economic price of oil will be like a decade after purchase—not in 2009 but in 2019. So how can the world get better when Detroit systematically makes it worse?

Answer: Detroit must simply stop producing defective, "reverse leak," oil-dependent cars. This does not mean a push for better gas mileage. Better mileage standards are illusory, because they function the way filter tips do on cigarettes. The world must get off of oil for all the reasons broadcast nightly. Moderating an addiction is not kicking an addiction.

Detroit must be reformed. But no reformation can commence until the country recognizes Detroit's special code words of deception, distraction and dissimulation. Listen carefully when anyone in the car industry utters any one of these three key phrases to explain why they have not delivered better alternative fuel vehicles: 1) "We need infrastructure," 2) "There is no market demand," and 3) "We are awaiting new technology."[1]

HONDA GOES SLOW ON THE CIVIC GX

Home-based or community-based fueling is one of the answers to energy independence, not trading a petroleum needle for an ethanol needle or a CNG needle. During the first decades of the automobile, in the early 20th century, there were no gas stations. The network Ford and Edison tried to create for their electric car in 1912 was designed so home-based wind turbines and small kerosene generators could recharge the batteries. This home generation was to be augmented by overnight recharging in local garages connected to the local electrical utility and slim streetside "Electrants" to be as common as parking meters. Unfortunately, the electric car was subverted by the very company that actually controlled the technology, the Electric Vehicle Company. That company thought it could make more money selling less efficient but more ostentatious and muscular internal combustion machines.

Now America is witnessing a similar subversion by one of the best and most enlightened car companies in the world, by the company with some of the most dedicated executives and innovative engineers, by the company that makes the car this writer personally drives, by the company that has boldly offered the promise of fuel independence to America but turned its back on its own promise and potential. The company that has disappointed most is the Japanese firm, Honda. They have done it in part by falsely using the code phrase: "No infrastructure."

Honda's CNG vehicle, the Civic GX, has been dubbed the "greenest car in America," by the American Council for an Energy-Efficient Economy and other environmentally conscious groups. Honda's GX became a *cause célèbre* for many alternative fuel devotees because it held out the prospect of true energy independence by detaching from the gas station umbilical cord. Not only does the GX achieve good equivalent mileage of approximately 24 MPG with a range up to 220 miles, the vehicle uses no gasoline, just common natural gas. Most importantly, the GX was designed to work with a compact home refueling unit called the Phill, made by a company called Fuelmaker. The home refueling device after tax credits would only cost a few thousand dollars and pay for itself as the user was weaned off oil. The dynamic benefit of the Honda GX was a non-oil consuming vehicle that could connect to a supply line as easily as any home grill or any other gas appliance.

Then a clear and present solution to oil dependence suddenly began to go bad. First, the vehicle was deliberately made less attractive. Honda has earned a reputation for outfitting its cars with some of the finest audio systems and GPS navigation units on the highway. But these were not available with the GX. The stereo was whole steps behind gasoline-based Civics. Nor was GPS available.

Then, consumers from California to Florida began going public with horror stories about trying to install Phill units in their home. In many cases, the installation could not be done. Customers complained they were treated shabbily. Most extraordinarily, Honda inexplicably refused to sell the car in most states. Most Honda Civic GX cars were sold in just two states, California and New York, and those in large part were to small fleets.

Fuelmaker, manufacturer of the Phill, also refused to sell the home refueling unit to most of its existing dealers for other CNG products. Ironically, at the same time, Fuelmaker aggressively sold the refueling appliance in France through Gaz de France, in Italy through Alpengas IMI, in Switzerland through Holdigas, in Poland through GZOG, in Finland through Gasum Energiapalvelut Oy, in the Czech Republic through Milox and Vitkovice Cylinders, in the Netherlands and Belgium through Teesing, and in Lithuania through SG Dujos. In China, Fuelmaker sealed a five-year $65 million distribution deal through CornerStone International Trading Company at a special ceremony, clicking wine glasses with photographers snapping pictures. Indeed, by spring 2008, Fuelmaker had sold about 3,000 of its easy to use Phill units worldwide. About two thirds of those were sold in France.

But only 300 Phill units were sold in the U.S., as of spring 2008. Fuelmaker's dealer support website for the Honda Civic GX shows dealers in only two states, California and New York—even though Honda enjoys about a thousand thriving dealerships around the country.

Who controls the stock of Fuelmaker and the distribution of the Phill? Answer: Honda does.

Officials at Spokane Community College were amazed when Honda refused to sell the school a small fleet of the Civic GX cars, either directly or through local dealers. Spokane sits on a major natural gas line. School officials and city leaders became convinced they could become a proud regional epicenter in the national movement to get off oil by systematically switching their school-owned vehicles to CNG. Students and faculty could join in. The ideas were first outlined by this author during a series of 2007 speeches advocating a "Green Fleet Initiative." School enthusiasm prompted interest by the Spokane city government as well.

Proponents envisioned Phill units installed at the school and at city locations to be shared with the public, and then quickly adopted by home users. This would follow the same technology as personal computers which migrated from corporations to homes of employees and then back to widespread commercial use. Eventually local alt fuel enthusiasts planned to convince the local Postal Service, as well as the large UPS and Fedex hubs, to switch to CNG. Integral to the idea was Spokane's training a bright cadre of CNG automotive mechanics to service the Civic GX. Graduates of the mechanics program could not only service locally, but they could fan out and export their expertise around the nation. There was talk of turning the entire city into a CNG vehicle zone accenting both home and shared neighborhood refueling which would gradually move Spokane away from oil.

Oil switch organizers in Spokane spoke of expanding east and west to create a CNG corridor stretching from Denver to Seattle. Spokane Community College supporters then hoped to replicate the movement in other community colleges, the perfect sponsors for such regional initiatives. Greg Stevens, human resources director for the college and one of the spearheading personalities behind the CNG fleet idea, quipped in an email, "For us, this potential partnership is a no-brainer."

What happened? Why did Spokane's ideas never get beyond the talking stage?

Answer: Honda refused to sell the cars—not even one. Despite months of phone calls and emails with senior Honda alternative fuel executives, partial starts and false starts, Honda CNG officials declined to meet with Spokane officials or even say yes to the sale of a single vehicle. Dealers in Spokane answered that they simply could not get the cars from Honda. After about ten months of frustration, the idea simply died.

A Honda executive in charge of CNG and GX development was

asked point blank, "Is your company even interested in selling these CNG cars as fast as you can to as many as you can? Are you enthusiastic about this vehicle?" His answer: "No comment."

Honda can revel in congratulations and accolades from the green movement because the Civic GX and the Phill independent refueling device represent a potential turning point in the effort to kick the oil addiction. But throughout the CNG vehicle advocacy community, Honda is snickered at and quietly ridiculed for its refusal to proliferate its own alternative fuel vehicle. The company continually repels the urgings of eager consumers and the CNG industry, claiming there is no infrastructure to refuel the car, that is, few CNG gas stations—even though the car was designed to be home refueled. Honda also claims there is no demand for the automobile. It declines to advertise the vehicle to consumers or permit sales to those who manage to learn of it on their own.

"They are amazing," lamented one long-time CNG vehicle advocate during a late August 2008 interview. He added, "Honda makes so much hay about its CNG car, but they don't want to sell them."

Honda is not the only company that refuses to sell its CNG cars. General Motors dwarfs Honda's refusal. GM manufacturers as many as 19 different CNG vehicle models around the world, as of summer 2008. Indeed, as of 2008, the company was still introducing new models, including luxury editions, in India. GM has successfully sold many of the natural gas vehicles now driving the roads of Asia, South America and Europe, although precise figures are not available. On July 31, 2008, GM Vice President of Research & Development, Larry Burns, bragged in a company blog, "GM already has extensive experience with natural gas vehicles. Our Opel Zafira CNG is among the leaders in Europe, where gasoline and diesel fuel are costly." When another GM vice president in charge of alternate fuels was asked why these vehicles were not sold in America, he stated, "no demand."

Ford also sells natural gas vehicles throughout the world, competing with GM. Once again, the company refuses to manufacture the vehicles in America except as demonstration projects. A senior Ford executive attending a taxi fleet conference in Seattle was asked why the company denied America the same vehicles it sold elsewhere. He dodged the question, answering, "My goodness—we're just trying to stay alive, just trying to stay in the game." The Ford fleet official's reference was to the company's dire financial condition—attempting to stave off bankruptcy following customer defections. When asked publicly, Ford claims there has been "no demand" for CNG vehicles or other alternative fuel vehicles in America.

Ford has repeatedly stated it will go slow on advanced alternative fuels. In November 2007, CEO Alan Mulally surprised the LA Auto Show and automotive writers with vague references to starting "a discussion" about alternative fuels, and iffy references to alternatives in 2012. CNet's review of the LA Auto Show was typical in labeling Ford's stance as disappointing. "On the subject of alternative fuels, Mulally was more vague," stated CNet, adding, "While Ford may talk the green talk, it's important to note that the company is among the automakers opposed to CAFE (Corporate Average Fuel Economy) standards that would require a company's consumer line of cars, when combined, to offer average gas mileage of 35 MPG by 2020."

HONDA WITHHOLDS ITS HYDROGEN VEHICLE

Honda again achieved alternative energy limelight with the roll-out of its sleek and stylish hydrogen fuel cell vehicle, the Clarity. Boasting kinetic body styling, an exquisite interior, *par excellence* handling and roadability, the Clarity is a feat of automotive engineering. Most remarkably, the car uses no petroleum. Instead, its fuel cell uses hydrogen reformed from natural gas or electrolyzed from water. Hydrogen can also be made through a bacterial reaction, and several laboratories are trying to improve the yields.

In 2005, Honda insisted its advanced hydrogen car would not be ready for the first consumers until 2012. As rapid progress was made on the vehicle's technology and design, the release date was steadily advanced until Honda premiered its dazzling Clarity at the 2007 Los Angeles Auto Show, promising a summer 2008 availability. The vehicle was rolled out as promised. But to the disappointment of many, only a few Clarity vehicles were actually produced, these leased to specially selected personalities in the Los Angeles area. Honda has stated it only plans to produce a few hundred more between 2007 and 2010. "Basically, we can mass produce these now," admitted Kazuaki Umezu, in charge of Honda's Automobile New Model Center in Japan, where the FCX Clarity is built. "We are waiting for the infrastructure to catch up."

But like the Civic GX, the Honda Clarity was designed as a home-fueled vehicle. For years before the rollout, Honda's hydrogen car, then known as the FX, was pictured in advance promotions as a vehicle connected to a box, a little larger than a backyard air conditioner. That box is Honda's Home Energy Center, designed to "reform" ordinary household natural gas, providing the electricity needed to run an entire home as well as fuel at least one hydrogen vehicle. Like the CNG car, the hydrogen vehicle was designed to require no public infrastructure.

Where is the Home Energy Center? The device has been developed by Plug Power of Latham, New York, which specializes in advanced hydrogen technology. But Plug Power's device is controlled through a strict licensing agreement with Honda. A Plug Power manager at the National Hydrogen Association's 2005 convention in Washington D.C. stated that the Home Energy Center could be made somewhat more compact but was good enough to go into mass production within months of receiving the go-ahead. He stated that the only thing holding the product back was Honda, which controlled the license.

By 2007, it was clear that Honda was consciously going slow on the development, deployment and sale of the Home Energy Center. In promotions, the company began omitting references to the essential home fueling component of its sleek new hydrogen car. Instead, the company emphasized the new need for metropolitan filling stations—a fueling infrastructure— which it rightfully claimed was years in the making. But this was the exact opposite of what they had committed to when they developed the car and its companion Home Energy Center.

When asked, Honda officials began cryptically claiming the product was "not ready." Yet efficient hydrogen devices are readily available in Tokyo and stacked outside Tokyo households to generate residential electricity. By deliberately going slow on the Home Energy Center—the very device designed to create individual freedom from infrastructure—the highly-regarded Japanese carmaker has essentially laid out a decade-long phase-in for the vehicle and ensured that more than 99 percent of the United States will have no access to its hydrogen vehicles for years to come.

In early 2008, a senior Plug Power manager with day-to-day involvement with the Honda refueling device told this reporter. "It works well. It's running well. But it is Honda's call." In late summer 2008, a Plug Power staffer involved with the project, repeated the assertion. "It works fine the way it is," he stated, "What year it comes out is Honda's call. Please call Honda."

When asked, yet another Plug Power official stated, "If Honda accelerates the program, we will accelerate it. If they don't, we can't."

Certainly, any home refueling center will be improved over time, like cell phones, computers, televisions and automotive technology. But the mass deployment of the Home Energy Station seems to have simply been withheld.

Why would Honda hold back on its own marvelous technology? Japanese Honda has understood that if it mass produces the Clarity and Home Energy Station, the public will flock to it as fast as they have been fleeing from Honda SUVs and similar gas guzzlers. While Honda makes some of the most fuel-efficient and well-engineered cars in America, the Japanese company also makes gas guzzlers, such as the Honda Ridgeline crossover pick-up which only achieves about 15 MPG in the city, the snazzy S-2000 sports car at 18 MPG, and the Pilot midsize SUV at about 16 MPG. In July, 2008, sales of the Pilot, manufactured in Alabama, posted a 47 percent drop over the previous year, just 7,486 compared to 13,136 in July, 2007. Pilots were down more than 21 percent for 2008. Sales of other Honda gas guzzlers plummeted as the market for such vehicles by all makers completely collapsed in mid-July, 2008. When the market for SUVs collapsed, SUV leasing programs by numerous auto companies nearly all terminated during a several-day period in July, 2008.

Even Toyota, maker of the most coveted fuel-efficient gasoline-powered car in the nation, the Prius hybrid, suffered a 12 percent sales drop in July 2008, driven by a 27 percent drop in its truck and SUV sales. Ironically, even Prius sales fell 8 percent because Toyota refused to make enough to satisfy demand, claiming it could not detect a growing market for the highly desired hybrid leader. Throughout 2008, Prius-hungry buyers often placed their names on four-to six-month long waiting lists, thereby delaying any car purchase at all, hence the overall Toyota drop.

Helping America and the world out of its financially wracking oil addiction would hamstring overall profits for the Japanese carmakers. In the case of the Honda Civic GX and Clarity, the company may have indeed gone slowly on its best alternative fuel vehicles, keeping them out of America's anxious hands, for no reason other than the preservation of profits on gas guzzling vehicles well into the third decade of the 21st century. Honda cars, generally among the best built in the world, boast a scrappage rate that can easily exceed a decade. Vehicles sold in 2009 and 2010 can be expected to require parts and service for at least a decade. A parallel dynamic is the knowledge that as the nation flees the gas guzzlers of GM, Ford and Chrysler, they will flock to the more fuel efficient Honda models, such as the Civic, the Accord and the Fit. Hence, Honda can dominate the fuel efficient category while keeping its customers on oil.

Although Honda is holding back its hydrogen car using the well-worn "infrastructure" canard, hydrogen vehicles operating with either internal combustion engines or fuel cells have been created by GM, Ford, BMW, and other manufacturers. Each of the majors has developed its version of this cleanest car. GM hopes to mass produce hydrogen cars for the Chinese market as soon as possible. But hydrogen is scheduled to be kept from American purchasers for years to come.

Claims that alternative fuel technology does not exist are also wearing thin on a world that now knows electric cars were invented in 1835 and dominated the roadways before the World War I. While battery technology can be constantly improved, electric vehicles represent an old technology waiting to be resurrected and powered by ever-more advanced batteries. The hydrogen fuel cell was invented in 1838. The first hydrogen bus was created in 1934. Hydrogen now powers at least five submarines in the German navy. For years, scores of hydrogen city buses have been operating in at least ten major European cities: Amsterdam, Barcelona, Hamburg, London, Luxembourg, Madrid, Porto, Reykjavik, Stockholm and Stuttgart, as well as in various American metropolitan centers.

GM AND ITS VOLT

Although some of the best carmakers, such as Honda, are going slow on their best solutions to the oil crisis, there is hope. The fast approaching electric vehicle surge by a number of carmakers seems to be scheduled for a 2010 arrival when a group of newly sprouted automotive battery factories is expected to be ready for unprecedented mass production. This output will enable production of thousands of electric cars by a plethora of manufacturers large and small.

True, in 2010, several auto manufacturers are planning to rush to market with bright new electric cars, especially those which can be recharged at any common electrical outlet. But the best and most genuine hope for kicking the oil addiction with a mass produced electric car comes from a most unlikely candidate, from the company that has done more to hurt America than any other auto manufacturer, from the company that headed up a criminal enterprise that helped systematically destroy electrical trolley transit throughout the nation, from the company that consciously helped Adolf Hitler murder millions, from the company that worked so diligently to keep the world dependent on petroleum all these decades, from the company that in the face of looming bankruptcy, decided to reinvent one vital portion of its decaying empire and perhaps make a down payment on repairing the great damage it has wrought to the nation. That company is General Motors.

GM, pummeled by its failures but still powerful for sheer magnitude, has promised to pull out every stop and drive full speed toward electrification. They promise to begin with the Volt. At first, the Volt project was justifiably denigrated by electric car aficionados as little more than yet another GM ploy to garner distraction publicity for a concept car the corporation had no intention of producing. But in mid-2008, as sales for GM's gas guzzlers slid off a cliff, and as GM rushed to rally $15 billion in capital to quell rumors everywhere of impending bankruptcy, the Detroit giant boldly bet its teetering future on the electric car. The Volt is not designed to be a pure electric car, like the Nissan-Israeli project or like the Tesla Roadster. Rather, the Volt will come equipped with a flex-fuel engine to charge the batteries and extend its range beyond the 40 miles provided by an average charge.

Electric cars are so simple and possess so few moving parts, that they need very limited service beyond tires and rotation, and battery replacement. Hence, the electric car potentially outmodes a pivotal profit center for the automotive industry: parts and service. But by adding a flex-fuel internal combustion engine to create a sort of occasional plug-in hybrid, GM hopes to retain at least some semblance of a replacement and service market for the engine parts that can be expected to wear out. Since the average automobile in America travels between 25 and 35 miles per day, the Volt's gasoline function may never be engaged by most, especially for urban commuters using the Volt as a second car. But the internal combustion engine—which can run on any form of ethanol from corn to sugar to cellulosic in blends up to E85—would be utilized on such common longer trips. Dozens of other everyday journeys exceed 40 miles, such as commuting from the south side of Chicago to the far northern suburbs, shuttling up and down the length of South Florida, transiting through the Southern California metroplex, driving north and south along Colorado's Front Range, and traveling anywhere in Texas. For this reason, GM calls the Volt, an "Extended Range Electric Vehicle." The Volt approach actually makes sense.

GM has broken its promises for years and misled an entire nation about cars. But this time the company has been unequivocal, repeatedly leaving no room for retreat or even a wiggle. In a mid-July 2008 interview with this writer, GM vice president of global management, Jon Lauckner, was explicit. Beginning November 2010, Lauckner averred, GM would begin making as many Volts as it could, as fast as it could, with the hope of selling them as affordably as possible to as many who would buy them. Unlike Honda's restrictive approach to its CNG and hydrogen vehicles, GM promised to roll Volts off its assembly line by the thousands. Days after the interview, company executives, from the president to the publicist, began repeating the message to anyone who would listen. The message: GM would mass produce the Volt commencing November 2010. By mid-August 2008, approximately 35,000 eager customers had signed an *ad hoc* waiting list to purchase Volts as soon as the company's Hamtramck, Michigan plant released them.

Lauchner stated in the July 2008 interview that while it would take months to ramp up to full production speed, he expected to see tens of thousands of Volts cruising America's roads within the first year. Several weeks later, sensing the electricity in the air over the new car, Lauchner's spokespeople began using the broader term "electrification" to refer to much of the GM line. By late August 2008, GM declared that its rush to electrify was not just limited to the Volt, but would soon energize its heavier SUV models as well.

Electric car start-up companies abound. They are swimming upstream to reform an entrenched industry, fighting the odds, cautiously juggling financing, factories and physics. But since the first decades of the 20th century, no other company in the world has shown the ability and sheer manufacturing muscle to mass produce on the level that GM is capable of. After all, GM is the company that helped Hitler launch a motorized war, and then helped America rapidly mobilize to defeat him. GM can make the Volt happen. When they do, they will force other companies to follow suit. That is expected. In the wake of GM's highly charged Volt commitment, companies from Tesla to Toyota began revising their electric car strategies.

Tesla, for example, announced a practical departure from its six-digit price-tagged electric Roadster, asserting that beginning in 2010 it would annually build 20,000 affordable, multi-passenger Model S electrics, to be assembled near San Francisco. Toyota finally agreed to create a plug-in hybrid as so many had urged, also for 2010. Hyundai announced plans to create a propane-electric car by 2009, premiering it first in Korea.

GM can spearhead a movement to mass deploy electric vehicles. But electric will not be king. Producing a million Volts leaves 250 million other gasoline-burning vehicles. GM cannot save the day by itself with its Volt. But the company can be a leader in the movement to reform oil consumption. If the project comes to fruition, the Volt movement will be a redemptive moment for a new GM. As a GM spokesman told me after a discussion of the company's dark past, "I wish we could rewind the tape of history." History cannot be rewound. But it is possible to fast forward into the future. GM may be doing just that.

RETROFITTING AND THE OPEN FUEL STANDARD

Electrification is enticing, but it will take years to make an impact. Yes, by the end of 2010, heads will turn as the occasional electric car drives by. But it will take all of 2011 before the sight of an electric car becomes commonplace. A measurable impact will probably not be seen until 2012 and beyond. In the event of an oil interruption, the country will be unable to wait four to five years to see a difference.

As of August 2008, tens of thousands of unsold SUVs and other low mileage vehicles have been crowded into parking lots awaiting a buyer willing to endure a decade of escalating oil prices. In an oil crisis, or perhaps before, those should be upfitted to flex-fuel immediately. Consumers would then find them attractive.

The same principle should be applied to new cars being manufactured. Numerous assembly lines were either temporarily or permanently shut down during mid-2008. The downtime for these plants would be an ideal opportunity to cheaply and dynamically convert all new production to flex-fuel. The cost of the modification would be no more expensive than the vehicle price giveaways Detroit has found ineffective.

Mass adoption of a flex-fuel approach means the "Open Fuel Standard" which requires car manufacturers to make their cars capable of operating on a broad spectrum of fuels and propulsion systems. The "Open Fuel Standard" immediately relieves a dependency on oil and can be accomplished, experts argue, for as little as $100 per new vehicle. Indeed, the Open Fuel Standard legislation introduced in 2008 enjoys tri-partisan support—Independents, Republicans and Democrats—in both the House and Senate. The bill mandates that carmakers adopt the Open Fuel Standard approach for 50 percent of all their vehicles by 2012 and 80 percent by 2015. Some of the most conservative members of Congress believe that requirement is economically and environmentally reasonable. There is no need to wait until 2012. It can be done now.

PREMATURE SCRAPPAGE

A key obstacle to getting off oil is the "installed base" of about 250 million gas consuming vehicles that guarantee continued dependence upon oil for years to come. Complicating that predicament is that the older car and truck models achieve some of the worst mileage on the road. The answer: destroy them or, to use the industry term, scrap them.

Mandatory or voluntary scrappage programs are commonplace, designed to retire the most fuel-inefficient and environmentally unfriendly vehicles, often in exchange for governmental cash support. In the past, vehicles older than 15 years have been targeted by various governmental and community programs. But under *The Plan,* all vehicles over 10 years of age, not upfitted or otherwise exempted as collector vehicles, would be subject to mandatory scrappage. In such programs, the engine is typically destroyed and the other parts salvaged. Starting this program during an oil crisis would immediately target the oldest cars first. Scrappage programs have long been advocated by policymakers, but too often opposed by auto interests.

Congress proposed a scrappage provision as part of the Energy Policy Act of 2002 that would help states carry out their own mandatory scrappage of cars and trucks older than 15 years. The stated goal was to achieve better overall fuel economy and emissions. Section 803 of the 2002 legislation, "Assistance for State Programs to Retire Fuel-Inefficient Motor Vehicles," would have taken hundreds of thousands of gas guzzlers off the road and compensated owners. But the Automotive Services Association, which represents the repair industry, seeing a gold mine in patching up old vehicles, lobbied vigorously against the provision. Eventually, the federal program was watered down into a quiet, strictly voluntary program and stuffed into an innocuous corner of Section 832. It was quickly forgotten.

Similar programs have been opposed in numerous local American jurisdictions. A scrappage measure in Vermont, Senate Bill 316, was defeated by the auto hobbyist community in 2007. The Florida Governor's Action Team on Energy and Climate Change included vehicle scrappage in a May 2008 review of the state's options to improve transportation, but the measure has yet to be implemented. Yet, as many as 13 million vehicles annually are voluntarily scrapped each year by their owners, according to Polk Co., which tracks new registrations and scrappage rates.

However, Canada has inaugurated a program to take effect in 2009. "Of the 18 million personal vehicles in use in Canada, an estimated five million are 1995 or older models," declares a Canadian government web statement. "These older vehicles were not manufactured according to today's more stringent emissions standards, and produce 19 times more smog forming air pollution than newer vehicles. Although they make up less than one-third of vehicles on the road, older cars generate as much as two-thirds of the smog-forming pollutants caused by personal vehicle use."

The Canadian national legislation is based upon numerous well-proven provincial and local Canadian programs, many with user-friendly names such as "BC Scrap-It" and "Cash for Klunkers," both in British Columbia, "Steer Clean" in Nova Scotia, and "Car Heaven" in Alberta. Accelerating scrappage will be good for the move off of oil, and will encourage upfitting or production of newer alt fuel vehicles.

PATENT AND LICENSE INTERVENTION

Improving automobile performance and alternative fuel has long been plagued by calculated patent sequestration and the use of restrictive licensing agreements, too often designed to keep good technology suppressed. Critics of the auto establishment like to talk about the advanced battery designs, alternative fuel systems, nano-technology and other technical accomplishments sequestered by energy and automotive companies for the sole purpose of keeping them off the market.

Indeed, the history of the automobile throughout the 20th century is a chronicle of punishing patent litigation and abuse, designed to obstruct competition and keep good products off the market. The infamous Selden Patent, a bogus patent for an allegedly primitive automobile, was contrived in the 19th century to stop independent automakers. Controlled by the Electric Vehicle Company, the Selden Patent was used to keep Henry Ford from producing his cheap Model T during the first 11 years of the 20th century. Similarly, battery patents were endlessly litigated to thwart competition. Even the late 19th century bicycle monopoly—corporate precursors to the 20th century electric vehicle monopoly—cultivated the fine art of patent abuse and litigation harassment of people independently making and selling bicycles.

Under *The Plan*, an Energy Patent and License Intervention Office would allow government action to enable good energy technology to rapidly proceed in the marketplace. This office would be empowered, on public complaint, to investigate whether alternative fuel technology was being expeditiously deployed in the marketplace, or withheld. For example, such an office could examine Honda's license agreement with Plug Power for the Home Energy Center, or Fuelmaker for the Phill unit to determine whether the country could benefit from the more rapid deployment of the technology. Such an office could compel the patent holder to grant compulsory licenses so that the technology may be exploited for the sake of the country, and encourage competition. Under this scenario, a third party would be authorized to exercise the patent, but required to pay a fair fee to the original holder.

In other words, in a true emergency, if the technology was workable, the controlling company would be obligated to deploy it or see it deployed by another company. In everyday parlance, "use it or lose it."

The concept itself is a so-called "compulsory license." Such a license is an "exception" to patent law generally imposed by a court or agency of government to address a special crisis or inequity, failure to commercialize following government funding, abuse of patent or a wartime condition. There are several controversial precedents reserved for wartime, a health crisis or the technical advances of the digital age, but they have never been applied to a fuel crisis.

British Petroleum came into being when, during and after World War I, the Anglo-Persian Oil Company was empowered by the British government to take over enemy property. In this case, the enemy property was a German company operating in England, called "British Petroleum." Eventually, through various machinations, the same corporate hegemony allowed Britain to seize Turkish oil interest in Iraq.

The patents and trademarks of Bayer Aspirin were seized from Germany by the United States as enemy reparations after World War I. The German company did not regain the rights to its own patented and trademarked aspirin until 1994 when it purchased the American pharmaceutical giant, Sterling Winthrop, which had gained control of Bayer Aspirin. Thus, Bayer regained the right to its own product in the U.S. market.

Under the 2001 Doha Declaration of the Trade Related Aspects of Intellectual Property Rights Treaty adopted by the World Trade Organization, governments have the internationally recognized right to implement the "health emergency" provision and grant compulsory licenses for pharmaceuticals. Brazil and other countries have invoked this notion to produce AIDS medicines. The United

States has debated the same right in the event of an anthrax attack. The concept of a compulsory license has also been embraced by the Copyright Office for certain dramatic and musical performances to be webcast where the rights are withheld. Courts provide this remedy where a market injustice justifies it.

Section 308 of The Clean Air Act provides that the EPA Administrator may ask the Attorney General to certify to a federal district court that a patent holder be ordered to license a patent to a third party under terms and conditions determined by the court if various conditions are met. Legal experts say these conditions include: that the patent is necessary for compliance with the standards of the Clean Air Act, intended for public or commercial use but not reasonably available, that no reasonable alternatives to licensing the patent exist for meeting the specified standards, and failure to license the patent may cause reduced competition or monopoly conditions.

In a genuine oil emergency, where the safety and health of the public is at stake, freeing up dormant alternative fuel technology could be a justifiable tool to expediting the switch from oil.

THE GREEN FLEET INITIATIVE

But even with new technology implementation, mass upfits, and premature scrappage, a true fix cannot be achieved without the Green Fleet Initiative. The most important source to help the nation kick the oil addiction is not the White House or the state house but the country's major fleet owners. Carmakers such as Honda, BMW and Toyota are waiting for only one thing before they commit their considerable resources away from gasoline cars and toward hydrogen, electric, natural gas (CNG) or other alternatively fueled vehicles. Vehicle manufacturers want tangible demand. Fleets—governmental, commercial and private—have a compelling volume purchasing power no automaker can ignore.[45] They can generate hundreds of thousands of alt fuel vehicles.

For-hire carriers in 2004 operated 675,000 trucks. The top ten include such companies as UPS, Federal Express, and Yellow Roadway. UPS alone deploys some 100,000 brown trucks daily as it makes more than 13 million deliveries every 24 hours. Yet only slightly more than 800 of UPS's massive fleet ran on compressed natural gas as of Summer 2008. Within Federal Express's 70,000-vehicle fleet, the company operated 30,000 medium-duty trucks, of which less than a few hundred were hybrids, as of Summer 2008.

Some six million additional vehicles are owned by private commercial fleets such as Sysco, Wal-Mart, Halliburton, and Frito-Lay. Wal-Mart alone operates more than 7,000 vehicles that in 2007 drove 900 million miles. Verizon operated 70,000 trucks and cars in 2004. Waste Management operated about 28,000 vehicles in 2004. Krispy Kreme Donuts operated 750 vehicles in 2004. City, state, and federal agencies, as well as universities, comprise just a fraction of America's 38,000 private fleets.

If fleet managers adopted a Green Fleet Initiative, that is, a *hierarchy of purchasing* that mandates non-oil consuming alternative fuel vehicles with a preference for the most fuel efficient, the race would be on among all truck and heavy-duty vehicle manufacturers from GM to Mercedes to be the first to fulfill those orders. Volume purchasing would multiply and accelerate the technology, bring down costs, and migrate such vehicles swiftly from commercial fleets to average consumers.

Therefore, the public and environmentally conscious companies can choose to ship green, shop green, drink green, and even communicate green. For example, in choosing an overnight shipper, will it be Federal Express or UPS? In buying soda, will it be Coke or Pepsi? Corporate policies, such as nondiscrimination, labor fairness, environmental damage, and other conduct are already determining factors for many in choosing where to place their business. Therefore, there is more power in one petition to UPS and Federal Express than to all the members of Congress combined.

The government should revoke tax deductions for oil-only fleet vehicles, and replace them with tax incentives for alternative propulsions and fuels.

Ironically, the federal government maintains America's single largest fleet by far—more than 600,000 vehicles. Environmental groups have consistently sued the federal government to compel it to follow its own alternative fuel guidelines. The Energy Policy Act, passed after the first Gulf War, mandates all federal agencies to reduce oil dependence by ensuring that some 75 percent of new vehicle purchases use alternative fuels. The law has been largely ignored. A steady cascade of court rulings has rejected government requests for delays. Government purchases alone could spur the rapid adoption of any category of alternative fuel vehicle.

Many believe the notion that man inherits the earth. Not so. He only holds it as a precious legacy for succeeding generations. That inheritance must not be squandered or reduced to rubble because of the war, industrial epidemic, or ecocidal damage arising from the intoxicating but nonetheless toxic fumes of petroleum.

Until now, there has been no cohesive plan to cope with a protracted oil shut down. Now there is one. *The Plan* cries out for implementation before it is needed. If we wait until the day the oil stops, surely it will be too late.

Endnotes

CHAPTER ONE: THE PLAN

[1] "Rising Food Costs Further Pressure World Hunger," *The Wall Street Journal (WSJ)*, July 9, 2008. "World Entering a Danger Zone," letter, Robert B. Zoellick to Yasuo Fukuda, *World Bank News and Broadcast*, July 2, 2008. "Fuel Costs Cut Deeply into Food Aid," *US News and World Report*, July 7, 2009. "Food Price Controls Likely, Says UN," *Financial Times (FT)*, October 29, 2007.

[2] "FACTBOX: Food Price Rises Spark Protests," *Reuters*, May 15, 2008. "How the Rising Price of Corn Made Mexicans Take to Streets," *The Independent*, June 23, 2008. "El Salvadorans March against Hunger," *Spidered News*, May 26, 2008. "Food Riots Grip Haiti," *The Guardian*, April 9, 2008. "Addressing the Global Food Crisis," *Heritage Foundation Backgrounder #2131*, June 26, 2008. "Farmers Renew Protest in City," *Bangkok Post*, June 19, 2008. "The Looming World Food Price Crisis: Global Costs Have Shot up 57 Percent in Past Year, Says UN," *The Laval News*, June 26, 2008. "No Quick Therapy for Food Price Inflation Despite Counter-measures to Ease Pressure," *China Economic Net*, April 15, 2008. "India Tries to Avert Food Crisis," *Arab News*, April 2, 2008. "Australia Probes Soaring Food Prices," *Agence France Presse (AFP)*, February 12, 2008. "France to Double Aid for Food Crisis," *AFP*, April 18, 2008. "Feed the World? We Are Fighting a Losing Battle, UN Admits," *The Guardian*, February 26, 2008. "Gene modified Crops the Key to Food Crisis, Says Scientist," *FT*, July 7, 2008.

[3] "Warehouse Stores Restrict Rice Sales," *New York Times (NYT)*, April 24, 2008. "Citing Supply, Sam's Club and Costco Limit Sales of Rice," *The Washington Post*, April 24, 2008. "As Food Prices Soar, Some Shortages Appear," *CBS News*, April 23, 2008. Vermont Food Bank, "Federal Cuts, Increased Demand Squeeze Vermont Pantries," press release, July 8, 2007. "Care and Scare: Area Soup Kitchens and Food Pantries Could Soon be Out of Luck—and 'Real' Food," *Colorado Springs Independent*, July 3, 2008. "Supplies Dwindle at Food Pantries as Financing Bill Stalls in Washington," *NYT*, October 18, 2007.

[4] Gordon Brown, "PM Calls for Action to Deal with Food Crisis" (speech, London, April 22, 2008). "UK's Brown: Food Crisis is New Credit Crunch," *CNN*, April 22, 2008. "Biofuels 'Crime against Humanity,'" *BBC News*, October 27, 2007. "Food Inflation, Riots Spark Worries for World Leaders," *WSJ*, April 14, 2008.

CHAPTER TWO: CRUDE REALITIES

[1] Energy Information Agency (EIA), "Crude Oil Imports From Persian Gulf 2007," Report, April 10, 2008. Luis Guisti, Report, Senate Committee on Foreign Relations, June 22, 2006.

[2] EIA, "Projected Short-term Petroleum International Consumption," Report, Table 3a. EIA, "International Petroleum Supply, Consumption, and Inventories," July 2008. Ariana Eunjung Cha, "China's Cars: Accelerating A Global Demand For Fuel," *The Washington Post*, July 28, 2008. EIA, "World Petroleum Oil Demand 2004–2008," Report, Table 2.4, *International Petroleum Monthly (IPM)*, June 2008. EIA, "World Oil Balance, 2004–2008," Report, Table 2.1, IPM, June 2008. Also see author's interview with Source A, Department of Energy, 2008. See "Worldwide Demand for Oil Will Continue to Grow Rapidly," *Alexander's Gas and Oil Connections*, August 4, 2004. Also see "Asian Nations Driving World Prices," *The Regional Economist*, April 2007. Plamen Tonchev, "Rising Asian Oil Demand and Caspian Reserves: The Economic Debate," *Caspian Crossroad Magazine*, vol. 3, no. 3 (Winter 1998): 1–7.

[3] "World Oil Balance, 2004–2008," Table 2.1. EIA, "World Total Liquids Production by Region and Country, References Case, 1990–2030," Report, Table G1, *International Energy Outlook (IEO)*, 2008. EIA, "Chapter Three: Petroleum and Other Liquid Fuels," IEO, 2007.

[4] "Portable Power Generators: China Sourcing Report," *Research and Markets*, March 2006.

[5] EIA, "Petroleum Trade: Overview," Report, Table 3.3a, *Monthly Energy Review*, July 2008. EIA, "Petroleum Overview," Report, Table 3.1, *Monthly Energy Review*, July 2008. EIA, "Petroleum Products Supplied by Type," Report, Table 3.5, *Monthly Energy Review*, July 2008. EIA, "Petroleum Consumption: Transportation and Electric Power Sectors," Report, Table 3.7c, *Monthly Energy Review*, July 2008.

[6] EIA, "Crude Oil and Total Petroleum Imports Top 15 Countries," Report, May 2008.

[7] See generally Edwin Black, *Banking on Baghdad* (Hoboken, NJ: John Wiley, 2004), especially chapters six to nine.

[8] See generally Black, *Banking on Baghdad*. See also Christopher Pala, "China Pays Dearly for Kazakhstan Oil," *New York Times (NYT)*, March 17, 2006. "PetroKazakhstan Stockholders OK CNPC Bid," *China Daily*, Oct. 19, 2005.

[9] Canadian Association of Petroleum Producers (CAPP), "Canada's Oil and Gas Industry in the North American Energy Economy," *Canadian Oil and Gas Industry Outlook*, June 22, 2007. EIA, "Canada Energy Profile," June 16, 2008.

[10] CAPP, "2008 Crude Oil Forecast," Report, 2006. EIA, "Country Analysis Brief: Canada," May 2008. EIA, "Crude Oil and Petroleum Imports Top 15 Countries," Report, May 2008. International Energy Agency (IEA), "Monthly Oil Statistics: Canada Imports," Report, August 2007.

[11] CAPP, "Monthly Oil Statistics Canada Imports," August 2007.

[12] CIA, *The World Factbook: Italy*, March 10, 2008. EIA, "Table 3.12: Italy— Petroleum (Oil) Imports (Most Recent 12 Months)," Report, *International Pe-*

troleum Monthly, February 2008. "Monthly Oil Statistics: Canada Imports." EIA, "Table 3.9: OECD Europe—Petroleum (Oil) Imports (Most Recent 12 Months)," Report. *International Petroleum Monthly.* February 2008. EIA, "France: Energy Profile," Report, February 19, 2008.

[13] IEA, "Monthly Oil Statistics–for Canada, Imports." August 2007.

[14] Simon Romero, "Mr. Sandman, Bring Me Some Oil; Suncor Energy Is Turning Canadian Tar Into Energy," *NYT,* August 31, 2004. Author's emails and exchanges with CAPP, July 2008. Frank J. Atkins and Alan MacFadyen, "A Resource Whose Time Has Come? The Alberta Oil Sands as an Economic Resource," *Energy Journal,* vol. 29 (February 2008): 77.

[15] Argonne National Laboratory, "About Tar Sands," *Oil Shale and Tar Sands Programmatic EIS Information Center.*

[16] "Investors Decry BP's Entry into Tar Sands: Statement to be Submitted at BP Annual Meeting Today in London," *CRSWire,* April 16, 2008. Author's emails and exchanges with CAPP, July 2008.

[17] Environment Canada, "Acid Rain and the Facts." "Acid Rain A Growing Problem for Western Canada," *Science News.* August 16, 2006. Author's exchanges and communications with CAPP, July 2008.

[18] Gordon Laxer, "Freezing in the Dark: Why Canada Needs Strategic Petroleum Reserves," report, January 2008. North American Free Trade Agreement (NAFTA) Article 605a.

[19] See author's interview with CAPP, July 20, 2008. CAPP, "Crude Oil Pipeline Expansions and Proposals to the U.S. Midwest, Ontario, Québec and the U.S. East Coast," Report, Crude Oil Forecast, Markets, and Pipeline Expansions, Appendix C.1, June 2008. Author's emails and exchanges with CAPP, July 2008. Enbridge Confidential Internal Report.

[20] CAPP, "Canadian Petroleum Producers," 2007.

[21] See generally Gordon Laxer, "Freezing in the Dark: Why Canada Needs Strategic Petroleum Reserves," *CBC,* "The Current," February 6, 2008. Gordon Laxer and John Dillon, "Over a Barrel: Exiting from NAFTA's Proportionality Clause," report, Canadian Centre for Policy Alternatives, May 2008.

[22] "US Risks Trade Dispute With Canada on Fuel," *Financial Times,* February 15, 2008.

[23] "The Timing Is all Wrong for a Talisman Takeover," *The Globe and Mail,* May 27, 2008. "Canada Welcomes China's Cash," *Wall Street Journal,* August 20, 2005.

[24] See author's interview with CAPP, July 20, 2008.

[25] "Will Mexico Soon be Tapped Out?" *Los Angeles Times (LAT),* July 24, 2006.

[26] "Mexican Oil Production Falls 7.8 Percent in First Quarter," *Associated Press,* April 21, 2008. "Mexico Oil Output Drop May Spark Crisis," *Reuters,* June 14, 2007.

[27] "Carstens Says Pemex Can Meet Needs without Tax Cut," *Bloomberg,* June 21, 2007.

[28] "ENERGY-MEXICO: PEMEX in Death Throes Amid Political Squabbling," *IPS News,* February 26, 2008.

[29] "With Bombings, Mexican Rebels Escalate Their Fight," *NYT*, September 26, 2007.

[30] "Fire Breaks Out as Alon Reopens Refinery," *MSN Money Central*, April 7, 2008.

[31] Robert L. Bamberger and Lawrence Kumins, "Oil and Gas: Supply Issues After Katrina," Report for Congress, September 6, 2005.

[32] Minerals Management Service, Gulf of Mexico Region, US Department of Interior, "IXTOC Oil Spill Damage Assessment Study," March 1982.

[33] "British Petroleum Exploration (Alaska) Pleads Guilty to Criminal Violation of the Clean Water Act and Is Sentenced to Pay $20 Million in Criminal Penalties," *PR Newswire-USNewswire*, November 29, 2007.

[34] "Pirates Attack Oil Tanker off Somalia: Malaysian Watchdog," *AFP*, April 21, 2008.

[35] "Kuwait Still Recovering from Gulf War Fires," *CNN*, January 3, 2003.

[36] "Car Bombers Attack World's Largest Oil Processing Facility in Eastern Saudi Arabia," *Asharq-alawsat News*, February 24, 2006.

[37] Nawaf Obaid, Saudi National Security Net Assessment Project as cited by Khalid R. Al-Rodhan, "The Impact of the Abqaiq Attack on Saudi Energy Security," Center for Strategic and International Studies, February 27, 2006. "Abqaiq Facility at Heart of Saudi Industry," *AP*, February 24, 2006.

[38] "The Strategic Strait of Hormuz," *Oil & Gas Journal*, vol. 105, no. 28 (July 23, 2007).

[39] "Iran Tests Missiles in Persian Gulf, Hormouz," *AP*, July 9, 2008.

[40] "Attack on Abqaiq Oil Facility Foiled," *Arab News*, February 25, 2006.

[41] "Via Syria, The Making of Suicide Bombers for Iraq," *San Francisco Chronicle*, October 7, 2007.

[42] Robert D. Walpole, "Iranian Ballistic Missile, WMD Threat to the United States through 2015," Statement for the Record before the International Security, Proliferation and Federal Services Subcommittee of the Senate Governmental Affairs Committee, Washington DC, September 21, 2000.

[43] "Iran Readies Plan to Close Strait of Hormuz," *NewsMax.com*. March 1, 2006.

[44] "Foundations: The Underpinning," *Saudi ARAMCO World*, vol. 33, no. 6 (Oct–Nov 1982).

[45] "Exxon Shatters Profit Records: Oil Giant Makes Corporate History by Booking $11.7 Billion in Quarterly Profit; Earns $1,300 a Second in 2007," *CNN Money*, February 1, 2008.

[46] "Company Profile: Saudi Oil Co. (Saudi ARAMCO)," *Yahoo!*, December 2007.

[47] "Chavez Starts OPEC Summit with $200 Oil Warning," *AFP*, November 17, 2007.

[48] "Slouching Towards Petroeurostan," *Asia Times*, February 21, 2008.

CHAPTER THREE: A THIN ALLIANCE

[1] International Energy Agency (IEA), "About the IEA," www.iea.org/about/map.asp.

[2] Richard Scott, *History of the IEA: The First 20 Years*, Vol. 1: Origins and Structure (Paris: IEA, 1994), 45.

[3] Richard Scott, *History of the IEA: The First 20 Years*, Vol. 2: Major Policies and Actions (Paris: IEA, 1994), 71.

[4] Scott, *History of the IEA*, Vol. 2, page 86.

[5] IEA, *Saving Oil in a Hurry: Measures for Rapid Demand Restraint in Transport* (Paris: IEA, 2005). See generally IEA, *Oil Supply Security: Emergency Response of IEA Countries* (Paris: IEA, 2007).

[6] IEA, *Saving Oil in Hurry*. IEA, *Oil Supply Security*.

[7] IEA, "Hurricane Katrina: Summary of the IEA Response," *Oil Supply Security*.

[8] Scott, *History of the IEA*, Vol. 1, 116–118.

[9] Scott, *History of the IEA*, Vol. 1, annex. EIA, "US Stocks of Crude Oil and Petroleum," notes.

[10] Department of Energy (DOE), "Strategic Petroleum Reserve: Quick Facts and Frequently Asked Questions," www.fe.doe.gov.

[11] "Strategic Petroleum Reserve."

[12] "Strategic Petroleum Reserve."

[13] DOE, "DOE Announces Award of a Contract to Repurchase Heating Oil for the Northeast Home Heating Oil Reserve," *Fossil Energy Techline* (July 2003), www.fossil.energy.gov. See also DOE, "Northeast Home Heating Oil Reserve—Profile," www.fossil.energy.gov.

[14] Letter, President Franklin D. Roosevelt to Secretary of the Navy, March 21, 1942, quoted in DOE, *The Naval Petroleum and Oil Shale Reserves: 90 Years of Ensuring the National Security*, www.fossil.energy.gov/programs/reserves/npr/npr-90years.html.

[15] *The Naval Petroleum and Oil Shale Reserves.*

[16] See generally Edwin Black, "The Price of Prejudice," *Banking On Bagdad* (Hoboken, NJ: John Wiley, 2004). See also "Mixed Show," *Time*, June 23, 1941.

[17] "Strategic Petroleum Reserve."

[18] "Strategic Petroleum Reserve." DOE, *Annual Report*, 2006

[19] See generally Edwin Black, *Internal Combustion* (New York: St Martin's Press, 2006). Energy Information Administration (EIA), "World Nominal Price Chronology 1970–2006," *Annual Oil Market Chronology*. EIA, *Short Time Energy Outlook*. Jad Mouawad, "Oil Prices Take Biggest Jump in History," *International Herald Tribune*. June 6, 2008. EIA, "World Crude Oil Prices 1978–2008," August 6, 2008. WTRG, "Oil Price History and Analysis," *WTRG Economics*, www.wtrg.com, August 7, 2008. See Financial Forecast Center (FFC), "Financial Forecast Center's Historical Economic and Market Data, Dow Jones," www.forecasts.org, July 03, 2006. EIA, "This Week In Petroleum," August 6, 2008. EIA, "All Countries Spot Price FOB Weighted by Estimated Export Volume (Dollars per Barrel)," *Petroleum Navigator*, August 5, 2008. FFC, "Crude Oil Prices, Part Trend, Present Value, and Future Projection," www.forecasts.org, July 11, 2008.

[20] "Ali al-Nuaimi, "We Will Raise Production when the Market Justifies It,'" *www.petroleumworld.com*, January 16, 2008. EIA, "Gasoline and Crude Oil Pric-

es," *Short Term Energy Outlook*, July 2008. See also International Association for Energy Economics. (IAEE), "Oil Price Shocks and the Macroeconomy: What Has Been Learned Since 1996," *The Energy Journal*, March 1, 2004.

[21] "al-Nuaimi, "We Will Raise Production." "Bush Concern Over High Oil Prices," *BBC*, January 15, 2008. "Saudi Oil Minister: Kingdom Will Raise Production Only If Market Justifies It.," *Asharq Alawsat*. January 15, 2008. Raid Qusti, "We'll Go By Market Demand," *Arab News*, January 16, 2008.

[22] John D. McKinnon, Stephen Power, and Neil King Jr, "Saudis Rebuff Bush on Oil," *Wall Street Journal (WSJ)*, May 17, 2008. AP, "Mid-East Trip, " *WSJ* news photo, May16, 2008. WSJ, May 16, 2008. DOE, "DOE to Defer Strategic Petroleum Reserve RIK Deliveries," *DOE Techline*, June 5, 2008.

[23] *International Energy Agreement Act*, Act 1976 no. 155, New Zealand, 1976. *Petroleum Demand Restraint Act*, Act 1981 no. 12, 1981, New Zealand.

[24] *Emergency Oil Stocks Act*, No. 189/1999, Czech Republic.

[25] *Act of 16 February 2007 on Stocks of Crude Oil, Petroleum Products and Natural Gas*, Act of 16 February 2007, Poland, cited in IEA, *Oil Supply Security: Emergency Response of IEA Countries 2007* (Paris: IEA, 2007), Annex III.

[26] Naoaki Kurumada, "Outline of Petroleum Stockpiling and Emergency Response in Japan," *IEA/China Emergency Response Seminar, Beijing*, December 2002, 9–10. Tatsuo Masuda, *Petroleum Industry in Japan*, (Tokyo: Petroleum Association of Japan, 2007). Tatsuo Masuda, "Energy Policy Making: The Japanese Experience" (lecture, CGEMP, University of Paris-Dauphine, 14 February 2008).

[27] Author's Interview, Source B, 2008.

[28] Author's Interview, Source B1, 2008.

CHAPTER FOUR: THE FIRST RESTRICTIONS

[1] David L. Greene and Nataliya I. Tishchishyna, *Costs of Oil Dependence: A 2000 Update* (Oak Ridge, TN: Oak Ridge National Laboratory, 2000), 1–3.

[2] Edwin Black, "The Plan against Oil" in *Internal Combustion* (New York: St. Martin's Press, 2006).

[3] Edwin Black, *Banking on Baghdad* (Hoboken, NJ: John Wiley, 2004), 272.

[4] Black, *Banking on Baghdad*, 280.

[5] Black, *Banking on Baghdad*, 289–290.

[6] Black, *Internal Combustion*. Edwin Black. 2004. St. Sarkis Charity Trust, "Calouste Sarkis Gulbenkian," www.saintsarkis.org.uk.

[7] Duane Chapman and Neha Khanna, "An Economic Analysis of Aspects of Petroleum and Military Security in the Persian Gulf," *Contemporary Economic Policy*, vol. 19, no. 4 (April 2000), 3.

[8] House Committee on Foreign Relations, *Foreign Soverign Wealth Funds, Oil, and the New World Economic Order*, testimony by Dr. Gal Luft, May 21, 2008.

[9] "Gas Prices around the World," *CNN/Money*, http://money.cnn.com, March 2005.

[10] Peter Wilson, "Venezuela's Oil Sales to U.S. Drop as Chavez Sends More to Asia," *Bloomberg*, www.bloomberg.com, July 12, 2006. Cesar J. Alvarez and Stephanie Hanson, "Venezuela's Oil-Based Economy," *Council on Foreign Relations*, www.cfr.org, June 27, 2008.

[11] "Gas Prices around the World." "Venezuela Will Not Raise Gas Prices," *Associated Press (AP)*, June 27, 2008.

[12] "Chavez Warms of Huge Oil Price Hikes," *Reuters*, July 14, 2008. "OPEC Warns War With Iran Would Cause 'Unlimited' Oil Price Hike,"*AP*, July 12, 2008.

[13] "Energy Statistics: Oil Consumption (most recent) by Country," *NationMaster*, www.nationmaster.com, June 14, 2007.

[14] Mark Preston, "GOP Urges Price-gouging Probe on Gas," *CNN*, www.cnn.com, April 25, 2006.

[15] Salvatore Lazzari, "The Crude Oil Windfall Profit Tax of the 1980s: Implications for Current Energy Policy," Congressional Research Service (CRS) Report for Congress, March 9, 2006.

[16] *Emergency Oil Stocks Act*, No. 189/1999, part 64, and Amendment 560/2004, Czech Republic. Resources and Networks Branch, Energy and the Environment Group, New Zealand Ministry of Economic Development, "Discussion Paper: Options for Government Response to an Oil Supply Disruption," September 29, 2006.

[17] Franklin D. Roosevelt, "Establishing the Petroleum Administration for War," Executive Order 9276, December 2, 1942.

[18] EIA, "Weekly Petroleum Status Report," EIA-0208 (2008-32), data for week ended August 1, 2008.

[19] DOE, "Department of Energy Response to Katrina," fact sheet, September 2, 2005.

[20] DOE, "Department of Energy Gas Price Watch Reporting Form," http://gaswatch.energy.gov.

[21] Joint Economic Committee of the U.S. Congress, "The Promise of Alternative Automotive Fuels and Technology," study, December 2006.

[22] "Saudi Arabia Rebuffs Bush on Oil Production, *AP*, May 16, 2008.

[23] EIA, "World Oil Transit Chokepoints," report, January 2008.

[24] EIA, "Bio-fuels in the U.S. Transportation Sector," report, February 2007.

[25] Cargill Corporation, "Cargill History," www.cargill.com. Nicolas de Roos, "Examining Models of Collusion: The Market for Lysine," *International Journal of Industrial Organization*, vol. 24, no. 6 (November 2006), 1083–1107.

[26] Edwin Black, "The Corn Ethanol Deception—How Politicians and Agribusiness Tried to Silence the Critics and Promote a Bad Idea," *The Cutting Edge News (TCEN)*, www.thecuttingedgenews.com, May 5, 2008.

[27] Crowley Maritime Corporation, "Container Shipping to Central America and Cuba from the US East Coast," www.crowley.com.

[28] "Chevrolet Unveils New Avalanche with E85 FlexFuel," *GizMag*, www.gizmag.com, February 12, 2006. "Mitsubishi Launches Flex-fuel Vehicle (FFV) Pajero TR4 in Brazil," GizMag, June 26, 2007.

[29] Stagecoach Group, "Stagecoach launches UK's first Bio-Buses," press release, October 26, 2007.

[30] Philip Reed and Mike Hudson, "We Test the Tips," *Edmund's*, www.edmunds.com. November 22, 2005.

[31] Holli Estridge, "NuRide Launches Car-pool Program," *Bryan-College Station Eagle*, August 7, 2008.

[32] The Road Information Program, "Paying the Price for Inadequate Roads in Michigan: The Cost to Motorists in Reduced Safety, Lost Time and Increased Vehicle Wear," report, May 2007.

[33] E.H. Pechan and Associates, "Analysis of the Effects of Eliminating the National Speed Limit on NOx Emissions," report for EPA Office of Policy, Planning, and Evaluation, April 18, 2007.

[34] "Analysis of the Effects of Eliminating the National Speed Limit on NOx Emissions." "Fuel Economy Guide, Model Year 2007," report, DOE, Office of Energy Efficiency and Renewable Energy. Jad Mouawad and Simon Romero, "Unmentioned Energy Fix: A 55 M.P.H. Speed Limit," *New York Times (NYT)*, May 1, 2005. "Montana Code Annotated," 61-8-303, 2007. Jerry Gray, "The 104th Congress: Congressional Roundup; House Approves a Repeal of 55 M.P.H. Speed Limit," *NYT*, September 21, 1995.

[35] "Analysis of the Effects of Eliminating the National Speed Limit on NOx Emissions." Dave Montgomery, "55-MPH Speed Limit May Have Found Its Washington Patron," *McClatchy Newspapers*, July 11, 2008.

[36] Stephen L Oesch, "Statement before the Maryland House Environmental Matters Committee, HB 433 Automated Speed Enforcement," statement, Insurance Institute for Highway Safety, February 22, 2005. IEA, "Saving Oil in a Hurry," report, 2005.

[37] "Fuel Economy Guide, Model Year 2007." "Effects of Engine Idling," Lexington Health Department, State of Maryland, 2008. Clean Air Fleets, "Vehicle Idling Reduction Strategies," report, www.cleanairfleets.org, August 11, 2008.

[38] "Vehicle Idling Reduction Strategies." "Idle Reduction Technology: Fleet Preferences Survey," report, American Transportation Research Institute (ATRI), February 2006.

[39] Manav Tanneeru, "U.S. Cities Scrambling to Meet Rising Mass Transit Demands," *CNN.com*, July 16, 2008. Kenneth Musante, "Mass Transit Surge: Most Riders Since 1957," *CNNMoney.com*, June 11, 2008. Clifford Krauss, "Gas Prices Send Surge of Riders to Mass Transit," *NYT*, May 10, 2008. Ivan Moreno, "More Riders, Fewer Buses Mean Mass Transit Cuts," *www.Examiner.com*, August 2, 2008.

[40] Author communication with WMATA, June 13, 2008.

[41] Tony Bizjak, "Governor to Give Boost to Telecommuting," *Sacramento Bee*, www.sacbee.com, May 16, 2008. "Telecommuting Pilot Project," report, State of California, June 1990. Maureen Rousseau, "State Telecommute Group Pushes Fuel Savings Idea," *Hartford Business Journal*, www.telecommutect.com, August 11, 2008.

[42] Author interview with Recreational Vehicle Industry Association (RVIA), June 20, 2008. "Rising Gas Prices Cost Some RV Employees Their Jobs," FOX 13

(Tampa Bay, FL), July 14, 2008. EIA, "U.S. Vehicle Fuel Consumption by Vehicle Type: Household Vehicle Energy Use: Latest and Trends," Table A14, report, 2001. "RV Ownership Reaches All-Time High: Nearly 8 Million Households," study, University of Michigan and RVIA, December 6, 2005. "What's You Annual Usage/Mileage?," survey, *RV Park Reviews*, www.rvparkreviews.com, January 12, 2007.

[43] Author interview with Recreational Vehicle Industry Association (RVIA), June 20, 2008.

[44] Author conversations with various RV owners, June 20, 2008.

[45] Author interview with Recreational Vehicle Industry Association (RVIA), June 20, 2008.

[46] Author interview with Recreational Vehicle Industry Association (RVIA), June 20, 2008. "Winnebago Presents New Class B ERA," *Motorhome*, January 7, 2008.

[47] Author interview with American Boating Association (ABA), June 20, 2008. ABA, "Boater Education Requirements / Laws, ABA Boater Education Program," www.americanboating.org.

[48] EIA, "Residential Heating Oil Prices: What Consumers Should Know," brochure, January 2008. DOE, "Northeast Home Heating Oil Reserve, U.S. Petroleum Reserves," June 30, 2008.

[49] Department of Justice (DOJ), "Foreign Agents Registration Act (FARA) Information," www.usdoj.gov. DOJ, "FARA FAQ," www.usdoj.gov.

[50] "FARA Information." *Foreign Agents Registration Act*, U.S. Code, vol. 22, § 611 *et seq*, www.usdoj.gov.

[51] "FARA Information." *Foreign Agents Registration Act*.

[52] Project for Excellence in Journalism (PEJ), "PEJ Campaign Coverage Index: May 26–June 1, 2008," press release, June 1, 2008. Mosi Secret, "Obama Courts Tar Heel Support," *Independent Weekly*, April 23, 2008.

[53] See generally Black, *Internal Combustion*.

[54] Edwin Black, "Hitler's Carmaker," parts two and three, *The Cutting Edge News (TCEN)*, www.thecuttingedgenews.com, June 2008.

[55] See generally Black, *Internal Combustion*. Black, "Hitler's Carmaker."

[56] Black, *Internal Combustion*. Edwin Black, "Hitler's Carmaker," *TCEN*, part four, June 30, 2008.

[57] "Bill Takes Aim at 'Hummer Tax Loophole,'" *Your Money*, www.NPR.com, June 18, 2007.

[58] Author's conversation with Source V, 2007.

[59] Harold Pace, "Hummer History: How the Military's HUMVEE Went Civilian," www.automedia.com.

[60] "Bill Takes Aim at 'Hummer Tax Loophole.'" Bankrate.com, "The Hummer Loophole Gets Hammered," http://moneycentral.msn.com.

[61] Internal Revenue Service, Department of the Treasury (IRS), "Alternative Motor Vehicle Credit," U.S. Department of the Treasury, article, www.irs.gov, August 4, 2008.

[62] Green Car Congress, "GM Unveils Two Two-Mode Hybrids: SUV and Diesel Sedan," www.greencarcongress.com, January 9, 2005.

[63] Matthew Bandyk, "Subsidies and High Crop Prices," *U.S.News and World Report*, January 24, 2008. Joseph Hebert, "Group: Hydrogen Fuels Cells May Hurt Ozone," *www.Space.com*, June 13, 2003. Fuel Cells 2000, "International Hydrogen and Fuel Cell Policy and Funding," report, www.fuelcells.org.

[64] Edmund L. Andrews, "Big Oil Companies Reap Windfalls on U.S. Incentives for Drilling," *International Herald Tribune*, March 27, 2006.

CHAPTER FIVE: THE RETROFITTING REVOLUTION

[1] Author's enterprise and interviews with hydrogen experts, August 2008.

[2] Author's interviews with Karl Kordesch, 2005 and 2006. Author's interview with Hollinger Energy Center, August 2008. See also NASA Dryden Research Center, "Technology Facts—X-15," 2004.

[3] Author's interviews with Pat Grimes and Karl Kordesch, 2005 and 2006. "Saturn V: America's Moon Rocket," *Space Race*, Smithsonian National Space and Air Museum, www.nasm.si.edu. Danny Hakim, "An Electrovan, Not an Edsel," *New York Times (NYT)*, November 17, 2002. "Karl Kordesch," Institute of Chemistry, Hebrew University of Jerusalem, http://chem.ch.huji.ac.il.

[4] Author's interview with Hollinger Energy Center, August 1, 2008.

[5] Author's interview with Hollinger Energy Center, August 1, 2008.

[6] "GM Partners with Verasun and Shell for E85 Push in Chicago," *Green Car Congress*, www.greencarcongress.com, February 8, 2006.

[7] David Pimentel and Tad W. Patzek, "Ethanol Production Using Corn, Switchgrass, and Wood; Biodiesel Production Using Soybean and Sunflower," *Natural Resources Research*, vol.14, no. 1 (March 2005). David Pimentel, "Energy and Dollar Costs of Ethanol Production with Corn," *Hubbert Center Newsletter*, vol. 98, no. 2 (April 1998). Author's interviews with David Pimentel and Tad W. Patzek, March 2006.

[8] Pimentel and Patzek, "Ethanol Production Using Corn, Switchgrass, and Wood." Author's interviews with David Pimentel and Tad Patzek, March 2006. Hosein Shapouri, James A. Duffield, and Michael Wang, "The Energy Balance of Corn Ethanol: An Update," Agricultural Economic Report no. 813, Office of Energy Policy and New Uses, USDA.

[9] Edwin Black, "The Corn Ethanol Deception—How Politicians and Agribusiness Tried to Silence the Critics and Promote a Bad Idea," *The Cutting Edge News (TCEN)*, May 5, 2008. See generally Edwin Black, "Manhattan Now" in *Internal Combustion* (New York: St. Martin's Press, 2006).

[10] Jeremy Hackney and Richard de Neufville, "Life Cycle Model of Alternative Fuel Vehicles: Emissions, Energy, and Cost Trade-Offs," *Transportation Research, Part A*, vol. 35, no. 3 (43-266 (2001). Arthur W. Schwab and Everett H. Pryde, "Microemulsions from Vegetable Oil and Lower Alcohol with Octanol Surfactant as Alternative Fuel for Diesel Engines," United States Patent 4,557,734, 1985.

[11] Author's interview with Jonathan Lauckner, Vice President of GM, July 18, 2008.

[12] Author's enterprise, 2008.

[13] Elizabeth Rosenthal, "New Trend in Biofuels Has New Risks," *NYT*, May 5, 2008. Edward Niedermeyer, "First Ever Second-Generation Biofuel Plant Opens in Germany," *The Truth about Cars*, www.thetruthaboutcars.com, April 17, 2008.

[14] Author's enterprise with The Natural Gas Vehicle Association (NGVA), 2008 and CNG sources, 2007 and 2008. Wendy Clem, "5 Things You Need to Know about Using Home Natural Gas for Auto Fueling," *Green Car Journal*, www.greencar.com, August 15, 2008.

[15] Author's enterprise with NGVA and CNG sources, including Baytech, BAF, Trans-Eco, and Clean Energy, 2007 and 2008.

[16] Jesse Cogan, "Nissan and Better Place Promise Pure Electric—not Plug-in Hybrid—for 2010," *TCEN*, July 18, 2008.

[17] Author's interview with Evaira, August 2008.

[18] Author's interview with Evaira, August 2008.

[19] Author's interview with Evaira, August 2008. Chris Morrison, "Google. org Gives Electric Cars A Push, with Investments on Aptera and ActaCell," *VentureBeat*, July 23, 2008.

[20] Author's interview with BAF Technologies, July and August 2008.

[21] Author's interview with BAF Technologies, July and August 2008.

[22] Author's interview with Trans-Eco, July and August 2008.

[23] Author's interview with Trans-Eco, July and August 2008.

[24] Author's interview with Trans-Eco, July and August 2008.

[25] Letter, Trans-Eco to Customers, July 2008.

[26] Author's interviews Trans-Econ and BAF, July–Aug 2008.

[27] Author's conversations with car owners, April 19, 2008 and June 1, 2008.

[28] Author's conversations with car owners, April 19, 2008 and June 1, 2008.

[29] Author's interview with Trans-Eco, July and August 2008.

[30] Author's enterprise, July and August 2008. Author's interview with Source C, July and August, 2008.

[31] "What is the Effect of Ch. 380, F.S., Relating to Developments of Regional Impact, on Reedy Creek Improvement District," *Advisory Legal Opinion AGO77-44*, Attorney General of Florida, May 16, 1977. "How Crude Can They Get? Alaska Still Rolls over for Big Oil," *Earth Island Journal*, www.earthisland. org, September 22, 2004. See generally Black, "Manhattan Now" in *Internal Combustion*.

[32] Author's interview with Trans-Eco, July and August 2008.

[33] See generally Black, *Internal Combustion*. Tom Krisher, "Utilities Say Grid Can Handle Rechargeable Cars," *AP*, July 23, 2008.

[34] Author's enterprise with Honda Motor Co, Fuelmaker, Go Natural CNG, Natural Gasoline Vehicle Association, and GM, 2007-2008. Author's interviews with California GX owners, 2007–2008.

[35] Emily Le Coz, "Fry Fuel: McDonald's Franchisee Runs Cars on It," *AP*, March 14, 2006. Author's enterprise, Honda and GM, 2007-2008. Author's communications with McDonalds, August 2008.

[36] "EFuel100, Earth's First Home Ethanol System," EFuel100 Fact Sheet, E-Fuel Corporation, www.efuel100.com, 2008. Author's communication with EFuel corporation, August 6, 2008.

[37] Jim Saxton, "Iran's Oil and Gas Wealth," Research Report #109-31, Joint Economic Committee, U.S. Congress, March 2006. Gal Luft, "If Iran and Brazil Can Do It, So Can We," *The Cutting Edge News (TCEN)*, July 7, 2008.

CHAPTER SIX: FUNDING THE FIX

[1] Chris Isidore, "Exxon Mobil Sets Profit Record," *CNN Money*, http://money.cnn.com, January 30, 2006. Justin Blum, "Exxon Mobil Profit Soars 75%," *Washington Post (WP)*, October 28, 2005. Kevin Bogardus, "K Street Lobbyists Carry Water for OPEC," *The Center for Public Integrity (CPI)*, http://projects.publicintegrity.org. Steven Mufson, "Exxon Mobil's Profit in 2007 Tops $40 Billion," *WP*, February 2, 2008. John Porretto, "Exxon Mobil 2Q Profit Set U.S. Record, Shares Fall," *Associated Press (AP)*, July 31, 2008. See generally Edwin Black, *Internal Combustion: How Corporations and Governments Addicted the World to Oil and Derailed the Alternatives* (New York: St. Martin's Press, 2006). Kevin Bogardus and Bob Williams, "The Politics of Energy: Oil and Gas," *CPI*, December 15, 2003. Ronald Cooke, "What is the Real Cost of Corn Ethanol?" *Financial Sense Editorials*, February 2, 2007.

[2] Isidore, "Exxon Mobil Sets Profit Record." Blum, "Exxon Mobil Profit Soars 75%." Porretto, "Exxon Mobil 2Q Profit Set U.S. Record, Shares Fall." Mufson, "Exxon Mobil's Profit in 2007 Tops $40 Billion." Robert Pirog, "Oil Industry Profit Review 2007," *Congressional Research Service (CRS)*, April 4, 2008.

[3] IRS, "Alternative Motor Vehicle Credit," August 4, 2008. Bankrate.com, "Hummer Loophole Gets Hammered," *MSN Money*, http://moneycentral.msn.com.

[4] Justin Blum, "Senate Overwhelmingly Passes Energy Bill," *WP*, June 29, 2005. Erica Swisher, "The Real Cost of Oil," *Ethanol Today*, vol. 22, no. 44 (August 2005). CTA International Center for Technology Assessment, "Gasoline Cost Externalities: Security and Protection Services," January 25, 2005. David Gerard and Lester Lave, "CAFE Increases: Missing the Elephant in the Living Room," *American Enterprise Institute-Brookings Joint Center for Regulatory Studies*, June 2004. Senator Richard Lugar, "Energy Security: Cause for Cooperation or Competition," The Brookings Institution 90th Leadership Forum Series, transcript of proceedings, March 13, 2006 (Washington, DC: Miller Reporting Co., Inc., 2006).

[5] DOE and EPA, "Strengthen National Energy Security," *Fuel Economy*, www.fueleconomy.gov. LA Times Staff interview with T. Boone Pickens, "Pickens on His Energy Plan," *Los Angeles Times*, July 29, 2008. Waldo Proffitt, "The Saudi Arabia of Wind Power," *Herald Tribune*, July 26, 2008.

[6] Blum, "Senate Overwhelmingly Passes Energy Bill." Swisher, "The Real Cost of Oil." CTA International Center for Technology Assessment, "Gasoline Cost Externalities: Security and Protection Services." Gerard and Lave, "CAFE Increases: Missing the Elephant in the Living Room." Anthony H. Cordesman, "Outside View: The Costs of the Iraq War," *Washington Times*, December 14,

2004. Lugar, "Energy Security: Cause for Cooperation or Competition?"

⁷ Isidore, "Exxon Mobil Sets Profit Record." Blum, "Exxon Mobil Profit Soars 75%." Bogardus, "K Street Lobbyists Carry Water for OPEC."

⁸ Stephanie Mathieu, "Baird Says Use Stimulus Rebate Check on Green Appliances," *The Daily News (Longview, WA) Online*, www.tdn.com, March 26, 2008.

⁹ Jeanne Sahadi, How The Leading Democratic and Republican Presidential Candidates' Tax Proposals Could Affect Your Take-Home Pay," *CNNMoney.com*, March 22, 2008.

¹⁰ Robert Silva, "Inside the DTV Transition Converter Box Coupon Program," *About.com: Home Theater*, February 21, 2008. U.S. Department of Commerce, "Commerce's NTIA to Mail $40 Coupons Next Week," press release, *Commerce News*, February 15, 2008. Anne Broach, "Feds Unveil Digital TV Subsidy Details," *CNET News*, http://news.cnet.com, March 12, 2007.

¹¹ "The Bridge to Nowhere Abandoned," *CNN*, www.cnn.com, September 22, 2007. Sean P. Murphy, "Big Dig's Red Ink Engulfs State," *The Boston Globe*, www.boston.com, July 17, 2008.

¹² EPA, *Superfund 20ᵗʰ Anniversary Report*, updated September 18, 2007.

¹³ Civil Action No. A91-082 CIV, "United States of America vs. Exxon Corporation, Exxon Shipping Company, and Exxon Pipeline Company, and the T/V Exxon Valdez," and Civil Action No. A91-083 CIV, "The State of Alaska vs. Exxon Corporation, and Exxon Shipping Company," United States District Court, District of Alaska. Master Settlement Agreement, The United States of America and the Tobacco companies. See also Exxon Valdez Oil Spill Trustee Council, "Details of Settlement," www.evostc.state.ak.us.

¹⁴ Eliane Engeler, "Richard Branson: Airlines Should Pay Emissions," *The Huffington Post*, www.huffingtonpost.com, June 24, 2008.

¹⁵ See "Invasion," "The Nazi Intersection," and "The Price of Prejudice" in Edwin Black, *Banking on Bagdad* (Hoboken, NJ: John Wiley, 2004).

¹⁶ See generally Black, *Internal Combustion*.

¹⁷ See generally Black, *Banking on Bagdad*.

¹⁸ "Environmentally Responsible Mobility," press release, *Honda Media Newsroom*, www.hondanews.com, July 14, 2008. Greg Migliore, "Jamie Lee Curtis Gets Fuel-Cell Car, Likes It," *AutoWeek*, August 5, 2008. "American Honda Reports July 2008 Sales Down," *The Auto Channel*, August 1, 2008.

¹⁹ DOE and EPA, "FAQ," *Fuel Economy*, www.fueleconomy.gov.

²⁰ Samuel Johnson, *A Dictionary of the English Language*, s.v. "excise tax."

²¹ *The Columbia Encyclopedia*, s.v. "excess profits tax." William B. Paul, "Excess Profits Tax," *The Accounting Review*, vol. 27, no.1 (January 1952), 44–49.

Edwin Black, "The Taxi Cab Connection," *Chicago Monthly*, vol. 1, no. 1 (1974).

²² Stephen Schwartz, "The Hidden Costs of Our Nuclear Arsenal: Overview of Project Findings" in Stephen Schwartz, ed., *Atomic Audit: The Costs and Consequences of U.S. Nuclear Weapons since 1940* (Washington, DC: Brookings Institution Press, 1998).

²³ Schwartz, "The Hidden Costs of Our Nuclear Arsenal: Overview of Project Findings."

[24] NASA, "Project Apollo: A Retrospective Analysis," *NASA History*, http://history.nasa.gov, October 24, 2004. Public Information Office, Texas Department of Transportation, "Crossroads of the Americas: Trans Texas Corridor Plan," June 2002. Texas Department of Transportation, Minutes of Commission Meeting, June 27, 2005. Corridor Watch, "Challenging the Wisdom of the Trans-Texas Corridor," www.corridorwatch.org. Brad Foss, "Update 1: Experts: Alaska Pipeline Won't Solve Woes," *Forbes*, March 18, 2006. Alyeska Pipeline Service Company, "Pipeline Facts," www.alyeska-pipe.com. Jack Lyne, "Priciest Pipeline Ever," *Site Selection Online*, www.siteselection.com, January 17, 2005. New Airport Projects Coordination Office, "Cost Estimates," *Hong Kong Airport Core Programme*, www.info.gov.hk.

[25] "Details of Settlement." Anthony H. Cordesman, "Outside View: The Costs of the Iraq War," *Washington Times*, December 15, 2004. "Lawrence Lindsey, What the Iraq war will cost the U.S.," *Fortune*, January 11, 2008.

[26] Blum, "Exxon Mobil Profit Soars 75%." "Exxon Mobil Sets Record $11.68B Profit in 2nd Quarter," *AP*, July 31, 2008.

CHAPTER SEVEN: THE TRUE FIX

[1] This chapter is based on author's enterprise and interviews—both confidential and on the record—with corporate, consumer, governmental and industry association sources from 2006 to 2008.